ODONATA

Frequent flyer in the key of green

J.K. Oxford

Odonata Ink

ODONATA:

Frequent flyer in the key of green

Published in The United States of America

ISBN-13: 978-0-9847938-0-8 (paper)

ISBN-13: 978-0-9847938-1-5 (ePub/iPad)

Typesetting and layout by Ken Anderson

Cover art by Tom Trujillo Designs

The author wishes to express deep gratitude for generous permissions granted, by which the present work takes portions from the following literary treasures:

Beloved Master El Morya Khan's Wisdom
Agni Yoga Society
319 West 107th Street
New York NY 10025 USA

www.agniyoga.org
All quotes, except where otherwise noted are taken from:
Leaves of Morya's Garden Book II - Illumination. 1925

The World Teacher Trust-Global
Wasenmattstrasse 1
CH-8840 Einsiedeln
Switzerland
http://www.worldteachertrust.org

The World Teacher Trust-India
45-40-36/1, Akkayya palem
Visakhapatnam, 530 016, A.P., India

MechonMamre
Song of Songs, English translation,
Jewish Publication Society 1917 version
http://www.mechon-mamre.org

Master El Morya Khan Speaks: Agni Yoga Books

Especially when the world is quaking from hatred it is indispensable to make haste in opening the ears of the young generation. Without realization of the significance of music it is also impossible to understand the sounding of nature... The song of waterfall or river or ocean will be only a roar; the wind will not bring melody and will not resound in the trees as a solemn hymn. The best harmonies vanish for the unopened ear. Can people accomplish their ascent without song? Can Brotherhood stand without song?
Brotherhood. 1937

To construct a bridge from the spirit to the Brotherhood was not so difficult, but to establish a normal link between the Brotherhood and the people is unspeakably difficult. Men, like parrots, repeat the remarkable formula, "Death conquers death"—but they do not consider its meaning.

Fearlessness is Our leader. Beauty is Our ray of understanding. Simplicity is Our key to the secret doors of happiness.

Song brings us health, and blossoms will heal wounds. Therefore, I say, happy are those who understand sound and color.

Certain plants exist as reservoirs of prana. The pine trees collect it as if in electric needles. And as a bond between heaven and the depths of earth, the earth is covered with living antennae which gather and preserve the true renewing element of the spiritual tissue.

The importance of world-wide cooperation can be demonstrated graphically, even to some readers whose spirits are like cockroaches sticking in corners. When the date strikes, even an ant may come as a messenger.
Leaves of Morya's Garden - Book 2 - Illumination. 1925

Sound and color are among the principal fiery manifestations. Thus the music of the spheres and the radiance of the fires of space are the highest manifestations of Fire.

Fiery World - Book 1. 1933

The music of the spheres and the hymns of nature are more easily heard by those whose hearts are full of love. Those who insist upon formulas for the heart, for love, for compassion, will not open their ears to higher harmonies.

An intensified harmony arises when all the strings of the heart resound. Do not take such comparisons as mere symbols; long ago We spoke about the eyes of the heart. Indeed, man sees through them, and hears with the ears of the heart. How could we exist without such senses?

Supermundane - The Inner Life - Book 1. 1938

Dedicated to
my stellar parents,
Bruce and Dorothy

Contents

Contents

Walk like lions,
but guard the little ones,
because they will help you to open My doors.
Have understanding!

El Morya

Prologue

The spirit, which acts beyond time, also cognizes beyond the limitation of numbers, and is able to cognize up to the fourteenth gradation of hearing, whereas on the earthly sphere one can attain only up to the ninth.

Before the astral body sets out there is an outflow from the vertebrae. The various nerve centers unfold differently, and the time comes when this difference must be normalized by rest, just as a tuned piano should not be touched for a while nor pounded with any metallic object.

El Morya

I learned the art of flying one Saturday practicing scales on our big Steinway Grand piano. Daydreaming while my fingers floated across the keys, I was drawn into the river of sound–a part of me flying into the currents, to some high octave, *very* far away. From that day on, I knew soaring on waves of sound would someday come in handy. Music has a magic about it; even the tiresome scales. I had found a key to something really wonderful, the piano! Forever after I would hold it to be a masterful medium for the fine art of flying.

Have you ever looked closely at that famous photo of Ignace Paderewski–his wild hair flying as he rips across his Steinway? Where does one gather such intensity, such endless improvisation, such whimsical invention? Is his genius endowed from his ability to enter *inside* the music, plunging into it so deep, the chords become one with his own myelin fibers? Was it the gorgeous sounds themselves that lifted his genius to the highest level of piano virtuosity? Such is the brilliance of sound: its innate capability of setting us to sail without any wind. Under the hands of a Paderewski or a Chopin or a Beethoven, the 88 piano keys become a *living* entity, possessing intelligence–a peerless emotive art form on which to paint immortal masterpieces without ever having to change the canvas.

The piano's soundboard parallels closely the physics of the human body: Beautiful chords and unifying rhythms–when intercepted by the senses and delivered through nerve fiber pathways–strike the body's finer sensoria in a kind of philharmonic resonance. The body's response?–a charge of radiant electronic light.

India, the ancient forerunner of the *true Initiatic Arts and Sciences* has, for at least five thousand years, used sound as a basis for their scientific researches. The sacred mantra serves a dual purpose as both art medium and scientific mechanism, with which they explored the mysteries of the cosmos. Composed of seed syllables, the mantra–when chanted by the adept–attracts sympathetic sound currents, vibrating at very high frequencies which, becoming affinitized, effect a nuclear bonding with the higher octaves above Earth. Sounding the *bija* syllables, the adept is both an *antenna* and *a tuning fork*–uniting his harmonics in perfect attunement with *akashic* sound–thereby merging sympathetically with the vibration of the cosmos. Attaining resonance with the cosmic stylus, the adept perceives subtle streams of reality–imperceptible by even the most sensitive modern scientific instruments.

The ancient *Arts and Sciences* relies on one instrument alone–the *DeLuxe* model of the body's light vehicle–the higher mind, the nexus of *Atma-Buddhi*. By virtue of the sixth and seventh principles of man, which vibrate at very high frequencies, the adept transcends earth's deflective currents. By means of his single-eyed focus the adept *sees* sound in its higher-frequency aspects–as light patterns, crystal lattices, matrices.

> *The light of the body is the eye: If therefore thine eye be single, thy whole body shall be full of light.*

The single eye, the *Eye of Shiva*, is the adept's portal into ultimate states of divine consciousness, through which he perceives the reality of nature: photonic light displays, energetic patterns. In the awareness that the body is simply a condensed state of energy– sluggish within earth's gravitational pull of karma–the adept uses unbroken rhythms of sound which, through his practice of atomic acceleration–he raises his energetic state to that of light matter: the *Atmic* state–the seventh principle, the highest of septenary man. Reaching high states of frequency, the adept now radiates as a living lighthouse, his aura supercharged in electronic *life*.

The ancients describe an acoustic mystery: The electronic spin around the nucleus–of a single atom or a blazing sun–generates a distinct sound, and that sound corresponds to a color. Among Pythagoras' inestimable contributions to science, the sage taught this correspondence, giving us mathematical proofs demonstrating that the musical ratios produce the visible light spectrum. Severely restricting all noise in his wisdom school, this "Son of Apollo"– in perfect silence–was able to reach up into the starry dimensions through his *DeLuxe* body instrument, through which he perceived sounds emanating from distant planets: the *Music of the Spheres*.

Pythagoras heard life vibrating. He also felt life vibrating–in its precise, native rhythm. The engineer's oscilloscope detects vacillating rhythms which disrupt the electronic circuit of his devices–alien frequencies, *artifact noise*. The waltzing human heart pulses in its native 3/4 time. Dissonant music and broken rhythms alter the heart's electronic circuitry, disrupting the flow of the waltzing conductor. *Artifact noise* reduces the carrying capacity of the intelligent heart.

All sentient life incarnates with a keynote–paralleling the miracle of the unique pattern in the snowflake. Whereas a seed nucleus reflects the exact pattern of the mature tree, man's *keynote* is not a genetic phenomenon: The keynote lives in the nexus of man's sixth and seventh principles–the *Buddhic mind* and the *Soul–the Atman*. The keynote is fructified by Self-awareness, acceptance and striving for its ultimate fulfillment. Something magnificent awaits us: the rainbow of our individuality! Our keynote–living at the nexus where the octaves of matter merge with the octaves of pure spirit–is that quintessence, the *Soul.*

It is with the piano keys that I bookmark my Odyssey, my *Ode*–my song through the octaves of life–for it was through those octaves that I first learned to fly to the heights. Following the ancients in fine-tuning my own soundboard, I *expected* to find the link to my *Buddhic* faculties–the organ of pure perception. I wanted to *feel* my body's fiber-optic strings resonate to pure truth. I hoped to *build* my own *DeLuxe* instrument, to find gnosis through fluidic correspondence. Most of all, I sought after the confirmation of correspondence with truth, awaiting the thrill that resounds within the intelligent heart.

Chapter 1   Odonata

Sound and flowers
become a necessity for further flights.
The sounds of life of the spheres
and the vital emanations of flowers
truly enter into the recipe of Amrita.

El Morya

Odonata: *Dragonflies and Damselflies.* Beneficial aquatic and semi-aquatic insects, dedicated predators of mosquitos and other swatters. With descriptive names like *River Jewelwing, Amethyst Dancer, Aurora Damsel, Royal River Cruiser, Painted Skimmer* and *Blue Dasher*—is it any wonder the iridescent spitfires captured my young heart?

Born in the year of the *Water Dragon,* I too began life as a naiad—in the fluid habitat of my mother's belly. Emerging from her amniotic pond, I also bore a disproportionate head-to-body ratio—lacking, however, Odonata's farsightedness and 360 degree field of view. Growing up a young water dragoness, I discovered parallels with the Odonata: I too became proficient in the hover maneuver and the vertical take off. Like my freshwater "helicopter" *friends*, Odonata and I came equipped with the secret of lift, rarely touching the horizontal plane of the earth. We both seemed to do our best work airborne, above the creation.

Metamorphosis—in its seasonal cycling and transformation—landed me closer to the horizon, bonding me with new sounds: the poetry of field and forest. Mountain heights and freshwater ponds I found to be the best places to go beauty hunting—together with the Dragonflies and Damselflies–which themselves struck me as pretty flying flowers. Along with birds, Odonata had a special talent for interrupting my search for botanical wonders. From the first days of childhood I loved nothing more than nose diving deep into flowers, powdering myself in pollen, thrilling at their colors. Each season my inner song intensified its message: Hold fast to the compass of green–my heart's quintessence.

Affirming fealty to *El Capitan*–the magnetic true north of my heart–I maintained my flowery course– inspired, full speed ahead. My heart's leonine roar left no question: Headstrong and enthusiastic, the greens-warded earth tones became my inner shield, my strength. My life. Alas, the easiest road was not mine to take, and many were the cross winds met with, easily discouraging the less determined traveler. But I counted three things in my favor:

An indomitable will to follow that which I loved,
An inner freedom to fly unobstructed to that love, and
An inner sense to follow the key of sylvan green;

I knew that green was the voice of my sacred labor.

Chapter 2   First Flight

With the eyes of a child
You must come out and see
That your world's spinning 'round
And through life you will be
A small part of a hope
Of a love that exists
In the eyes of a child you will see

Moody Blues, 1969

Ten tiny fingers glide effortlessly up and down the keyboard of the mahogany Steinway grand. Imagining water cascading down rapids, compulsory practice becomes play. The fingers know their way around the piano by feel, offering her choices. She sets the diminutive digits on automatic pilot, leaving her mercurial mind free to roam. Turning to the western window, her green eyes trace the heart-shaped ivy climbing great trunks of Eucalyptus. Taking in the drama of her eighth autumn windstorm, she hears the ripping and spewing of bark–in episodic gusts–throwing themselves offsite, in sharp thrusts. Turning from the window, her eyes rest on the illustration on her music book, sitting on the shelf just above her hands. She is attracted by the schoolchildren on the cover who are walking happily to their own piano lessons. Taking in the arrays of boy-girl pairs, she sees they form a triangular geometry. Tracing the geometric line all the way back to the boy-girl pair in the distant horizon, she becomes riveted to the rear point–a microscopic speck appearing as small as a vanishing star.

Curious, she zooms in on the nearest boy-girl pair whose eyes suddenly appear to be looking directly at her: eager, primed, perched at the ready. Surveying each child, she discovers that each child holds a book which replicates the exact image on her own music book: the same triangle of children holding books and–again–the same music book. A mild shock passes through her young body.

Concentrating fully now, her eyes stick like super-glue to the image of children with books in the triangle, forming in her mind a rapid response–books within books–the image shrinking, becoming Lilliputian within each smaller image that she follows inward. Her eyes begin a rapid sequencing of capture-and-digest, her mind building in momentum with each mirrored image projected: a repeating sequence of books within books, flowing inward, shrinking smaller and smaller. Electric signals pulse through her viscera; sharp tracers transmit signals to her vagus nerve in systemic preparation for the next visual message...

An otherworldly stillness comes upon her, a calmness prevails... As in a standing wave, her body becomes a single point, fixed on a fractal of time. Something inside of her easily joins up with the moving image, merges with it, vibrates with it, accelerates along within it... She merges fully within the energies, herself no larger than a particle moving in time with the traveling wave...Her eyes are locked on to the inward-moving image, itself propagating into particle-sized mirrors of books within books.

Affinitized, she enters into the involuting mirrors, her occipital processes bouncing involuntarily–*ping-pong*–back and forth to the replicating optical phenomena: Books merging into triangles; triangles morphing into pyramids; pyramids shifting into mirrors; mirrors dissolving into particles; particles forming a crystal lattice.

Completely absorbed, she has become subsumed into the kaleidoscopic matrix, cycling in rhythm with the involuting portal, itself expanding and contracting, breathing. Ever-merging, multiplying and dividing, minutia evaporate into a vortex and vanish. Mimetic, she has become an integral function of the trigonometric forms swirling inside her inner vision. She has become tantamount to a reciprocal multiplying the 1 to the many; the many merging back into the 1.

Nearing her mental saturation threshold, there is a gyrating, whirling sound–as in a flywheel. Gathering full momentum inside of her, electrons are flying, excited atoms are reaching top acceleration, when suddenly–all at once she gains entrée to a new plateau. Perfect stillness washes over her, phasing in a pleasant lift, buoyant. She is light as a feather, floating into a spiraling whirlpool. She moves deeper into the breathing portal – itself shape-shifting – morphing....Now it is throbbing with vital force. Time is warped–somehow time is slow *and* fast simultaneously! She cycles into infinitesimal, tiny points of light, fractals flowing in upon themselves, involuting geometrically into inner space. Accelerating to a pitch of super high frequency–from ground to a quantum state–she levitates like a block of bismuth.... She is having a *magnetic moment!*

Lost to all awareness of earth, she has traveled into a time tunnel, oblivious to the sounds and smells coming from the kitchen where someone is humming and baking bread, immune even to the now-raging gusts convulsing outside, thrashing Eucalyptus bark in temper tantrums–*rip! thwack!* against the living room window.

"Doing, Juee? I am not hearing you?"

She hears a voice, recognizes its tone. It is a voice she obeys. She takes inventory: Her body is quivering, her fingers lay flat on the keyboard, inert. Wafts of freshly-baked bread quicken her olfactory bulbs. "It is father's voice!" she gasps, bringing her extremities back under her motor control. Attempting to focus, she is caught between flashes of feathery weightlessness, concluding that she has not yet fully landed. Struggling, she summons her faculties.

"How long was I gone?" I whisper to myself, the soldier in me taking possession. Like quicksilver I revisit my flight, thinking of telling the truth: "Hey, Dad–you should have seen me, I went flying into a picture." Right! Wouldn't pass quarantine. Sounds more like a fairytale than a fairytale. He'd never believe me anyway. So, being a child of eight years–like all children who want to be loved and not ridiculed–I made up a story. I lied.

For years I retraced the aerial adventure, recalling the physical effects leading up to weightlessness: the trembling of my body, the sound of vibrations ringing in my ear canal, my spine tingling and my head rushing. One salient memory was the voice inside me telling me to have no fear of flying.

At eight years old I had flown out of my body and traveled–possibly into the future. At very high speed, I had ridden on fractals of a mantissa. Possibly, I glimpsed infinity. Absolutely I was presented to a station of super high frequency and zero-gravity. Most fortunate was my youthful, psychological state of expectancy: Because I had no fear, I offered no resistance. Resistance is that fundamental law of physics that alters energetic functions. Remove the factor of resistance and watch the potency of energy increase. Resistance is a factor that can obstruct knowledge: Had I resisted the intense experience, if I had succumbed to fear or doubt by the velocity carrying all those replicating images dancing in my eyes–I would have forfeited the practical execution of quantum mechanics.

No, the only thing I feared was ridicule. At that impressionable pupal stage, nothing quite equals the setback of disbelief from a parent–especially one whom you worship. Some might have called my piano book flight a miracle; the mass mind would have called me an illusory dreamer. My sisters would have said I was ready for the psycho ward. There was danger in sharing these secrets, so I held my tongue.

What I did not know that day of my virgin flight would become clear as time passed: I was about to become a *frequent flyer*.

Chapter 3   The Mallard

Green is the colour of the sparkling corn
In the morning when we rise,
In the morning when we rise.
That's the time, that's the time
I love the best
Donovan, 1965

Visions are as real as the phototelephone.
One may consider them more real than the physical world.
One may question only from which source they come;
but the spirit controls this.
To a good inquiry there will come a good answer.

El Morya

Greens and pinks captivated me from the time of my first giant bubble-bath, compliments of the eternal child in the family: that would be my father. A mechanical whiz, he jimmied the vacuum, reversing the device from suction to pressure blower and Yowsah!–that machine could really blow behemoth bubbles, taller than my head–restrained from overflowing only by the 6-foot-tall shower door. Many long hours did I study in that tub, examining hundreds of bubbles, luminous specimens–painted in exquisite, iridescent watercolors. Thrilled at a striking pink thread, I traced it as it swirled around the surface of the bubble, phasing from pink to rose, or thrilling as the green shifted to aqua. No two bubbles were alike–some lost their colors quickly while some kept intact. Amazed, I was determined to follow each candy-colored swirl to its final destination. Set on solving the mysterious mechanics at play, I had to learn by hard experience that bubbles have limitations: they make terrible lab specimens. In deep study in my bubble aquarium, no one made me get out of my heaven-on-earth until the bubbles were all gone.

Vivid flowers fascinated me. One afternoon, admiring a bed of brilliant ruby-red petunias in my neighbor's garden, I noticed a color flashing around the corolla. Curious, I began to invite myself over more often that summer, just to see it happen again. I found that, if I could look long enough at the petals and not lose my patience–a color would flash, casting a corona, lasting for as long as I could hold up under the strain. When I turned away there was still an aftereffect blush, an aureole of dazzling light that would persist for a few minutes, making everything else look a dull color. That first ruby petunia flashed a phosphorescent, bottle-fly green. I found out that red and pink petals gave off different saturations of green- to blue-green. Yellow and orange flowers flashed in varied gradations of blue. Blue flowers took me a long time to see flash but when they did, it was worth the wait for the yellow region of the color spectrum to glow. After years of flower gazing, I often still cannot find the patience to pick up the halo cast around white flowers or ultra-pale pastels.

I tried without success to show the flower halos to my friends. My Dad humored me–he didn't try very hard. With either my nose in a flower or my eyes admiring one, I found it impossible to contain myself, shouting for my father to come see a flower flash. Smiling sweetly, he would correct me: "Juee, your mind is imagining." Privately I named flower gazing my *"imagining"* and continued to practice the art, discovering that when I focused full-tilt into a flower, occasionally I would get a slight quiver the moment of the flash. It was so like the trembling I felt on my virgin flight which, I reasoned, also occurred while *imagining* in rapt attention on my piano book.

I wanted badly to share the miracles taking hold of my days, but alas I was too young to articulate the mechanics of flying into a music book or seeing flower halos. Perpetually misunderstood, only in a rare case or two were my discoveries taken seriously. Relegated to living silently with my miracles, a certain joy was growing stronger each time I looked at a flower–flash or no flash. I became a beauty hunter. The world became beautiful simply because I spent the greater part of my time absorbing the virtues of flowers. Flowers set my heart on fire and I could barely contain the conflagration. The mold was set: I had fallen deeply in love.

Inclined towards effervescence, withholding my passion was torture. I simply could not always stay mum. At times I just *had* to release, especially coming fresh from the garden. Overflowing with flower joy, broadcasting my fanciful *verbiage du jour*–my siblings could claim I sputtered incoherent jabberwocky. Even if my father wondered if I *had* been visiting Alice in her looking glass, his response was always accompanied by a loving smile: "Juee, are you letting your imagination run wild again? You are sounding kind of weird." At least his assessment was fair.

The same cannot be said when my eldest sister held court. She judged me a somewhat odd and hyperactive child, charging that my utterances amounted to "mangled marbles." Yes, I confess: My descriptions were childishly inchoate, but I protest–they never were quite as bad as the "obtuse flotsam" she later claimed, marking me–if not altogether a different species–at least an unrelated splice, muttering under her breath about a forced hothouse tomato that had lost something vital in the overheated push. Making it quite clear that my opinion did not count, she was adept at slicing my growing confidence down to the dregs. She could have taken out a patent on her style of ignominious adjudication–so clever was she in her assaults, always out of parental earshot. Often so subtle they did not register in my outer mind, her poisoned barbs dug deep enough into my subconscious to cause seeds of doubt to linger– that is, until I finally got my bearings. Secretly I nicknamed my naughty sister *The Mallard*.

Growing up the youngest of 4 girls, I was used as target practice. When the Mallard trained the sister next in line as her apprentice, meeting them both head-on was like venturing deep into the Mekong Delta, defending myself against land mines and shrapnel in enemy territory. Physical attacks were beneath their dignity; they had a more devastating weapon: the evil eye. The Mallard's apprentice mastered the evil eye, a deadly weapon–selfish, demeaning, dark. With four menacing laser beams focused on me, they could easily paralyze me by the double dose–their beams forcing entry, piercing straight into my heart. If that didn't do the job, they finished me off with the supercilious eyebrows, raised up in disdain. At these moments–defending myself against their electrifying killing field–I badly needed a surge protector. My only survival weapon was in my imagination: Pretending my body was a dirigible–an invisible airship–I commanded that it lift me up and away to safety from the harmful currents of sibling evil. Forced to learn early, I had to find courage under fire.

Oh, yes–how can I forget the subtle character assassinations? When I spoke, the Mallard had the habit of making eye contact with someone nearby who would then join her in denigrating me, often innocently. Her intention?–to give me a winter pruning all the way down to the ground, of course. With her amazing abilities in subterfuge, her converts often never knew they were being used–either because her perfected moves invited laughter, or perhaps because I held my tongue, trying to be strong. I must admit, the Mallard possessed great talent for maneuvering people without them ever realizing she was the mover–controlling people without their slightest awareness. A champion people manager, she was comfortable *only* in the role as commander-in-chief, the Alpha female, and I was–well, *she* would say I was the runt of the litter.

Ailing dogs know instinctively to leave the home of their master when death is immanent, not wishing to disgrace the home with their putrefying corpse. Too many times during my youth did I hobble away, dying these many horrible dog deaths–reeling in pain. Sometimes I remained in hiding for long periods, feeling friendless and unwanted. During this time, *otherworldly* visions were coming into my life–adding heightened awareness to my already nervous disposition–making my "dog deaths" excruciatingly painful. I told no one.

Keeping constant vigil at bedtime, I contemplated my sorry condition, finding slumber difficult to reach. I was not aware that I was praying: All I knew was that I felt abject loneliness and did not wish to share my pain with anyone I knew. Staring up at the ceiling into space, a series of shapes began to take form: Rotating clockwise around a circle, many small wads of paper began to form–wads of scrunched up waste paper–the kind you toss into the trashcan. Circling around a sphere, the scrunched wads, I noticed, had words written on them–a hint of words, so small they were not meant to be read. Sequentially–as a rotating wad reached the top of the sphere–it would catch fire, shrivel up and *poof!*–it vanished. This immolation scene returned for many months, always at bedtime.

I came to understand it was a method for recycling waste energies, harmful mental and emotional waste. The wads helped me to eliminate the pain I was absorbing into my body during the day. The wads were showing me a procedure for recycling waste energies back into the universal for repolarization. Like mental compost piles burning in ritual effigy–the wads performed a kind of ecological-biodegradation cycling. Returning as needed, the wads were my cleansing agents of mercy, keeping my mental and emotional house in order–a helpful reminder to eject harmful words that might otherwise set up long-term camp inside of me.

Linked to the paper wad era, another phenomenon began to make bedtime visitations. Popular reading for children at the time, this next vision was a reenactment of *Little Black Sambo*–the Tamil boy who comes across four hungry tigers and surrenders his clothes and umbrella so they won't eat him. The tigers end up chasing each other around a tree so fast they all melt down into nothing but a pool of butter. The lesson of this vision was more obvious.

Chapter 4   The Rose of Sharon

*Just as We watch over you, so do We watch the development of
children throughout the world from the cradle on, weighing their best
thoughts. Of course, spirit does not often reach its best development,
and the number of deserting ones is great, but We rejoice at a pure
thought as at a beautiful garden.*

*Therefore, do not be astonished that the Great Teacher repeats simple
sentences, because by fixing these thoughts We sometimes provide
opportunity for an excellent flower of spirit to become stronger.*

El Morya

Was it just my imagination or did I hear voices? Yes, I'm sure
I heard something like purring or humming. Sitting up, I
peek outside my bedroom window where the setting sun is only
minutes from passing out of sight. Seeing nothing unusual, I fix
my gaze a moment longer to admire nature's mass spectrograph
washing the sky in neon red, phosphorus lemon and xenon orange.
Laying back to watch the last vestiges of nature's *skypainting* before
the shadows close the day–I wait and I listen.

I hear it again. In the distance. Far away...now the sound is coming
closer, still faint. Humming vibrations become male vocalizations,
a solemn chanting. Voices form two separate words but I cannot
make them out. The protracted drone is moving toward me,
closing in now. I sense a presence in my bedroom...the chanting is
amplified... intense vibrations resonate as though originating from
inside of me. Everything unfolds into a rhythm, embracing me.
Why do I feel such a strong presence around me when I cannot see
anything?

Slowly, the silhouette emerges: Monks clothed in vestments of
roughhewn burlap slowly form in the flickering shadows of my
bedroom...Medieval monks clad in frayed cloaks I see positioned

in rows–perhaps three rows, 10 abreast–one row above the other as in a cathedral choir. How is it their faces are not visible and yet I see that they face me directly? Inexplicable! Where a monk's face should be, their cowls–of diaphanous fabric–have the mysterious effect of shading the faces. Searching the facial voids, I conclude their camouflage is intentional. Is it to keep from distracting me from the point of the vision? I watch again for signs, listening carefully, certain now the monks address me purposely, chanting, chanting, chanting... A vague outline slowly appears: it is a cowled priest, standing on a dais with his back turned to me. I never see the priest's face, yet his presence is unmistakable: vastly impressive, a primary force. Weighty. He is leading the monks in this utterly solemn chant. Finally I make out the words:

"...God child...God child...God child...God child...God child..."

"Are you speaking to me? Am I the *'God child'*"? I ask nervously after a protracted interval, embarrassed by the sound of my own voice. No response. Only the solemn drone of chant emerging from the silhouette. How surreal! Half doubting myself, I turn away from the vision to recalibrate myself, mentally–back to normal–turning again to find the vision just as before. Who is this Catholic priest leading his brother monks in chant? A saint? What does this have to do with me? Why are they calling me *"God child"*? I do not remember how much time elapsed before I dozed off, tranquilized by this bizarre "postcard from the edge".

Several weeks after the monks' visit three words echoed repeatedly in my ear: Coming out of thin air blew soft sendings of: *"Rose of Sharon"*, leaving its mark in my nascent, fragmented awareness. After all, *Rose of Sharon* was the name of a common flower, *Hibiscus syriacus*–so, to hear it whispered seemed not at all unusual. With such intense botanical inclinations, my open-door policy welcomed *all* members of the plant kingdom; not unusual at all to find myself *flower-whispering*–unconscious of the origins of my thoughts. Absorbed in their fragrance and radiance, flowers were daily teaching me who they really were. Preferring to be among them in their sylvan habitat, I was an apprentice, learning the language of flowers.

Alongside *flower language*, I developed a special *animal language*. For example: "Butch", the neighbor's dog I named affectionately: *'Feenee Boo-shee Berry'*. When in discourse with the German Shepherd–in order to build animal self-esteem–I coined phrases like: *'Dahd leed lid bop'*, which of course means: 'That's a sweet little baby'. The standard question whispered to all the 4-leggeds was: *'Hoy Stah Hoy-la?'*, which translates as: 'What is it, honey?' which, animals recognize–dogs especially–as a sincere concern for their welfare. My doggie words won me comedienne awards: I was honored to witness my second eldest sister repeatedly doubled over in spasms when hearing me speak doggie talk–a striking compliment, coming as it did from one with such poised elegance, who held her tall frame straight as a tower–somewhat like stiff architecture. Years later my designer friend assessed my sister smartly as one who "would make a good senators' wife."

Considering that my plant and animal languages were budding in full force, the echoes of *Rose of Sharon* I presupposed as simply another flower-thought, a word-friend that I picked up somewhere. When the echoes came in, I just went with it–*correction*–rather, they went with *me*. I correct myself because this particular word-friend, *Rose of Sharon*, lingered well past the norm: Like a hovercraft circling overhead, it kept popping in at odd hours for an abnormally long cycle.

One Sunday morning at 5:30 a.m. *Rose of Sharon* was *sent* into my ear, waking me from sleep. Without hesitation, I obeyed the momentous presence of inspiration, conducting myself in the following manner: Knowing my father sleeps very lightly, I tiptoed extra quietly–one slipper at a time–downstairs. Being an atheist, if he caught wind of what I was about to do, I would likely be the source of endless jokes about how his flower-crazy, tomboy daughter suddenly found religion. Under these conditions, with extreme care I set the stereo volume control to zero, slowly rotating back to nearly inaudible–scanning until I found the Catholic station: I was about to hear my first Catholic Mass.

"Hail Mary full of grace, the Lord is with Thee, Blessed art Thou among women and blessed is the fruit of Thy womb, Jesus."

I don't remember how many clandestine Sunday mornings I spent whispering the rosary that summer–laying on the carpet like a *Mantis religiosa* in prone position with my ear to the stereo speakers–but as long as the communion ritual went undetected, I wanted to continue feeling the high I received. An unmistakable trembling sensation presented itself when I said the Mass, making me wonder if other Catholics experienced these effects when they recited the decades or sang the *Pater Noster*. My several Catholic friends suddenly became more interesting. Secretly, I harbored an affinity with everything Catholic, noting which of my friends were of the faith–with a childish and fuzzy plan in mind. I wanted to touch statues of Jesus, I developed a childhood crush on him. Saying Mass continued only as a private ritual, however–I didn't relish the thought of a churchgoer questioning my gooseflesh on a hot summer day. In these early days of secret communion with Jesus, I held my tongue. I was already carrying more than a few secrets and, having suffered through years of sibling torture, I deemed that sharing the latest visit from medieval monks and the whispering *Rose of Sharon* would probably be over the top.

About this time–still in grade school–I received my most precious possession. My Mother gave me a necklace that she wore as a young girl. On a silver chain hung a small glass bead, the size and shape of a small marble–crystal clear, fully transparent– displaying a single mustard seed suspended inside. I loved it the moment I saw it, attaching nothing from scriptures; I would know nothing of the holy book for decades hence. Presenting the seed to me, my mother related nothing biblical, wisely allowing me to find my own meaning for myself. She simply said something very lovely, as was her way–about how the necklace had given her strength as a young child–strength to maintain cheer amidst her beloved father who lay in bed 15 years, paralyzed. My Mother's words–something about how faith grows large from very humble beginnings– stayed with me and, when reading Jesus' words in later years, it made such perfect sense:

> *I tell you the truth, if you had faith even as small as a mustard seed, you could say to this mountain, 'Move from here to there,' and it would move. Nothing would be impossible.*

Raised Methodist, my mother married a no nonsense, deep-thinking atheist. I don't recall her ever speaking of her belief system–she just lived her beliefs outwardly as the virtuous woman she was inwardly. Church is pointless for people like my Mother who require no such crutch to keep step with their inward call to grace. My Mother could have taught the art of grace, carrying inside her as she did, the solid virtues of tolerance and peace. Everyone who met my Mother spoke of her beauty and grace. I took after my father.

Thinking over my Mother's words on faith one morning, I pulled the mustard seed laying on my neck to my eyes. In admiration, I began *imagining* deep into the science of how a seed grows–struck by the miracle of life, of the vitality contained within such a small seed. Life within the womb or the ovary waits for the proper environment before coming forth. Thinking of the mustard seed stretching forth like my Mother's faith waxed big inside me, profoundly affecting me. Holding the suspended seed between my fingers–with her teaching in mind–I found my body becoming warmer, the longer I identified with its virtues. Loving the mustard seed necklace as I did, I began *imagining* becoming small enough to enter into it. Children quite naturally have no resistance to such thoughts as flowing fully into an ideal simply because it is a beautiful thought– knowing that love of virtuous beauty propagates more such beauty, relative to the intensity of thought and feeling held for such a thing. Because I loved my Mother's mustard seed and because I loved the beautiful miracle of seeds, and because I loved my Mother–intense inspiration began filling my soul. *Imagining* my heart merging with the little seed–I was absorbed into that love–easily entering myself into it. By the full impact of *LOVE*–stretching forth so large now–I felt that love enshrouding my little body–growing instantly as large as our house! It is this virtue at which children, in their innocence–free from all stultifying restriction, free from dogma–excel. Offering no resistance, I received at that instant a living impression of how faith operates, all from my Mother's mustard seed. It all seemed so simple.

A young mystic in the making, my unusual encounters, visions and whispers continued unabated. Not a child blessed with patience, I wanted answers. When they did not come, I lost touch with rosary recitations–spending my time with flowers instead. It would be decades before I learned of my past link with the Catholic church. For the time being I admired stories of saints. It was much later that I was introduced to such saints as Bernard of Clairvaux who, during the Middle Ages sponsored Hildegard von Bingen as counselor to the most powerful in Europe–including the pope–during an age of witch hunts. It was many years before I read Hildegard's wisdom teachings: A true visionary, the abbess composed music and wrote treatises on botany, natural medicine, zoology and natural history. No church could possibly tame *her*, the prophetess who dared to describe the nature of women's orgasm!

Chapter 5   Wheatgrass Manna

The pores of the plants are enlarged not only by the advent of new leaves and flowers, but also by the removal of dead parts. The law of Earth's nurture affords, through the antennae of the plants, the possibility of drawing out of this reservoir by means of smell and sight the precious quality of vitality, the so-called Naturovaloris, which is acquired through conscious striving

El Morya

Growing up in Hollywood in the 20s, my father became a champion seed hunter, riding his bicycle for miles in search of tree seeds–scavenging tin cans and starting his own little nursery. His lust for nature rubbed off on me, as did the telltale pollen adorning the tip of my nose. "Juee, you've been out pollinating flowers again" my Dad could be heard saying more than a few times. One of my first flower thrills was discovering that, when the potent lemony-smelling Southern Magnolia ovary matures–I could squeeze from the plump, red womb a silky latex thread which seemed to stretch out forever. I haven't figured out why these days I can draw out a silky thread no longer than my fingernail.

I don't recall one outing that my father went without imparting the *nose test*: nipping leaves and holding them to the nose, pronouncing the family linked with the particular fragrance. "When in doubt, use your snout" I would say later in botany classes. His nose tests came first, then came the mouth test–a test I was reluctant to master, even though I watched him chew and spit endless plant material without any physiological harm, concluding his practice served to inoculate his body against pathogenetic organisms. It was great fun to learn botany his way: aiding the memory by sensory linkage. How many times we chewed the ultra-sour stems of yellow-flowering Oxalis, *Sour Grass*, simply to enjoy the visual comedy chewing sour stems elicited–"turning Japanese" at every chance. He showed me nutritious, so-called "weeds", handing me a piece of edible *Purslane*, which is high in Omega-3 fatty acids.

Always he grew Crucifers: mustard, kale and collards, but he frowned on Chenopods, such as spinach and chard because their calcium oxalate crystals can tie up the body's calcium. The house was never without fresh fruit; oranges, grapefruit and bananas were staples. In his hot house he grew a year-round wheatgrass crop, which he alternatively called *Manna* or *Greeners*. Always frugal, he used Mother's sewing scissors for *Manna* harvesting, staining them grass-juice green for life. Same with our Osterizer which never did smell quite right after years of pulverizing wheatgrass. Improving the taste of his *Greeners* was not a priority–he simply strained the pulp and served the objectionable liquid up plain–so, when his clarion call went out announcing: "*Greeners!*"–I took a deep breath, held my nose and swallowed the stuff bottoms-up through the nauseating ordeal. Eventually he backed off force-feeding his chicks *Manna*, but he never stopped teasing me, my allergic reaction, saying: "Juee, Nebbah again!" Still to this day when I see, nay–simply *smell Greeners* at fashionable health food bistros, I am gripped by instantaneous gustatory revolt.

Holding a blade of wheatgrass, my father marveled at the perfection inherent in chlorophyll: "Chlorophyll's molecular structure is identical to our blood hemoglobin, except a difference of only one atom–an atom of iron in humans whereas chlorophyll has a magnesium atom" he would say. "*Only* from fresh greens can the body get complete vitamins and minerals–*only* nature can provide this. Synthetically manufactured vitamins are a total waste." I thought my father was amazing. I followed him around like a puppy.

Emphasizing the marvel of the *germ* encased within a seed, he held up a wheatberry kernel between his perfectly formed fingers and–gingerly dissecting the ovary–showed us the *germ*: "The germ is the essential part," he would explain, pointing to the colloidal casing, the embryonic plasma, naming the parts as he pared away deeper into the tiny vegetable foetus. "White bread," he stressed, "has zero food value because the germ is removed. See this oil surrounding the germ? It is rich in nutrients, but the oil becomes rancid and spoils the bread, so they remove the germ. White bread is a waste. It's *Pizon,*"(poison) he would say—of all processed foods. "Sling it," or "push away," he would say, gesturing seriously, prohibiting just about anything not natural—although there were times he could not resist the temptation of candy. With my ear perched always toward my father's wisdom, I hoped to gain entrance into his vast storehouse of knowledge. His ideas on science, nutrition and nature were gospel to me. He was the lynchpin guiding the young wheel of my life.

My father's mouth-watering wheat bread—baked fresh each weekend—sent billows of roasted grain-honey wafting through our house. In his old, white undershirt and blue jeans, his sinewy arms dug deep into the 100-pound burlap sack of *El Molino* wheatberries, each measure he poured into his cast iron *Corona* Mill. Always humming and joking, he could be seen every Saturday grinding away, producing wonderful vapors of freshly ground wheat grain. Working the dough with his hands—if there happened to be an audience gathered, my father never failed to entertain—and the neighbor children never tired of reruns either. My father would throw the sticky, yeasty mass up hard against the kitchen ceiling, drawing gasps from us kids, watching in breathless anticipation— the newbies gulping as the gluey blob began its first downward drooping descent. We followed the blob—stretching longer and longer until the gooey stalactite had reached its maximum limit. Acting nonchalant for high drama, my father would position himself some distance away until our screams demanded his return, to catch the falling dough. In one long glide—ala *Cosmo Kramer*— our hero steps in to save the helpless dough ball—barely clinging to life—from its fatal descent to the floor.

Forever testing some new invention, my father tried designing a more efficient packaging to preserve his bread. He worked on making a better contact lens until suffering second-degree burns and catching concern from my Mother. He concocted something he simply called "goop" to preserve piano hammers. He designed stanchioned lights that burned beautiful, colored flames from copper, magnesium and potassium-filled basins. A rational scientist who had studied veterinary science and chemistry at UC Davis, he was driven to discover truths for himself, often seen pouring through scientific journals and his beloved Merck Index–*the* encyclopedia of chemicals, drugs and biologicals. If you happened into his garage laboratory and asked him what he was doing, his standard answer was always the same: "I'm *gooping*".

Chapter 6   Grandparents

Hitler has only v'one ball
Goering is also q'vite small
Himmler is somewhat sim'lar
and Goebbels has n'er balls at all

Buckleigh Fritz Oxford

Buckleigh Fritz Oxford–"Buck"–That was my paternal grandfather. Buck's father had traded the German-Yiddish low country for American soil in the late nineteenth century, escaping to higher ground along with two million other immigrant Jews, changing the family surname at New York's Ellis Island.

Therese Van Grove–That was my paternal grandmother. Therese's mother, Jen Goldstein, had likewise been whisked from Budapest, Hungary, to the U.S. where she met and married my great Grandpa Jack Van Grove, whose family emigrated from Holland, and whose surname also was modified during the passage through the New York turnstile.

Great Grandma Jen–the archetypal domineering mother–had her sights fixed on grooming her young daughter to become a child starlet. The formidable Jen insisted on taking her only child— already professionally trained in dancing and drama at age ten— away to New York, a whopping three thousand miles distant from her father, Jack, in California. Jack was smart, tough and successful in the Steinway Grand piano business he owned in Beverly Hills, but he was no match for Jen, who ruled at home. Jen whisked her child off to New York, became her daughter's manager and watched proudly the payoff as Therese performed in stage and motion pictures with her new name: "Therese VanDevere".

As often happens, a man came along and changed everything. Therese was 14 when she met Buck, falling head over heels in love with the dashing and mustachioed screen writer, ten years older. It wasn't long before Therese and Buck were ripe to make a life together–alone. But Jen had built a solid rampart around her daughter and would defend it to the end; her daughter's career was blossoming and Jen was not about to let some handsome stud wreck her plans. Anticipating her mother's allergic reaction to the idea, Therese knew there was no escaping her mother's wrath once apprised of their nuptials–so the young couple decided it best to first make a clean break from captivity and ask forgiveness later, after the dust had settled. They eloped. Quietly packing their things, the love birds married en route to their new home in Hollywood where they continued their careers as screen writer and actress.

They had chosen the safest plan–Jen's prowess was legendary. Stories were told and retold how Jen could manipulate cars at busy intersections, insistent that she *alone* was entitled to squeeze past tangled traffic jams during the New York rush hour. Hungarians love jewels and Jen was often heavily bangled in gold bracelets. Driving her Lincoln convertible with the top down, she was known to engage in traffic control with her arms–laden with bangles dancing and clinking–flailing high in the air, furiously signaling wayward cars with her Hungarian mannerisms. Adept in traffic control at New York crossings–Jen Goldstein must have been a sight to behold.

It was never clear just how soon after the elopement the Mother-in-law meeting took place. Sometime after Jen's return home to Jack in Pacific Palisades, there was a knock on the door. Always the noble gentleman, Buck sincerely wanted to pay honor to his new Mother-in-law and to make reparations for damages. Painfully aware that in Jen's eyes he was perceived as the thief who had stolen her precious child prodigy–he was wary. His intuitions were correct: Jen was still fuming hot at the terrible betrayal, letting Buck have a double dragon-dose of her hot steam. Meeting Buck at the doorstep, Jen lurched at him, wielding a broom menacingly over his head. Her temperature rising–she made brushing sweeps with her weapon. Driving home the point that she would never forgive him, she flailed her broomstick and threatened his head–curses him in her native Hungarian tongue.

Both Buck and Jen were natural comedians, with very strong personalities, eventually becoming as close as two *Alphas* can. Anger doesn't last long when children arrive on the scene: My father was born two months before Therese's 16th birthday–the lovechild of the happy union. Neither Buck nor Jen lived beyond my second birthday but their Yiddish trademarks did. Buck's original creations were mainstay favorites at family gatherings, when my uncles would hold theatre in exaggerated Yiddish accents, reciting Buck's limericks and jokes–retrieving the comic genius of his mind, bringing the rhythmic poetry of his Yiddish soul in very close.

By default, when Buck passed away young, my Great Grandfather Jack became my "Grandpa". As a wee girl, I cherished Sundays when he treated us four girls to scrumptious Jewish delicatessen food. Dressed to the nines, Gramps picked us up in his polished, yellow 50s Cadillac. Unfortunately for passengers, seat belts were invented *after* the power brake. Being thrown forward suddenly as Gramps' foot was getting adjusted to the novel braking engineering–the Caddy's abrupt stops made for a bloody lip or two en route with our beloved chauffeur.

In honor of Grandpa Jack, my father allowed us these exceptions to his strict rule against eating red meat. I'm grateful for that because I've never found corned beef or Jewish Rye bread of the quality it had back then. Returning us home, Grandpa rested comfortably in the rocking chair in our den, beer in hand. A vigilant sentry, I worried about him during his catnap, unclear why his beer never did slip his grip. But I was too preoccupied to keep an eye out for his Budweiser, busy setting up my stage to entertain no less than my King. Madly moving furniture an inch this way or that, it was an amusing spectacle to see the little tot multitasking–as usher, stage manager and performer–fussing in juvenile haste, making ready my Sunday performances for King Grandpa Jack.

"All right, funny face, I'm ready for the show!" Grandpa yawned. *Funny Face* is all he ever called me–it was years before I learned its basis on fact: As a little tot with a skinny body, my head was created as a substantial dome–prominent in its juxtaposition–and emphasized by the tight ponytail which popped out–bird-like–on top of the rotunda.

At showtime, I grabbed a yellow and pink floral scarf, completing my simple outfit–which consisted of only pink underpants and black tap shoes! Throwing back the folding doors, I bowed to my audience before beginning my Sunday song-and-dance recital. In between the giggling I managed to sing and tap-dance the old favorite *Tea for Two*–never once conscious of the fact that I was dancing almost completely naked. It was hardly my nakedness that interrupted my performance that Sunday: I heard someone tapping at the den window and spied two uninvited pop-eyed orbits above a nose smushed flat up against the glass, looking inside. Recognizing the intruder as a neighbor boy, I panicked. The story goes that I froze in momentary horror and quickly bolted off the stage, shrieking several octaves above middle C–setting off a cascade of sympathetic canine alarms around the neighborhood. However, that was not the highlight most often recalled at dinner parties: Beyond the comical image of the little imp with the big head, dancing in pink panties and tap shoes–was the signet sealing the memorable exit: I ran for my life offstage, awkwardly contorted with a firm, two-handed grip–holding in protective custody *only* the most valued possession–my bellybutton.

Chapter 7   Jewish Passover Seder

The serpent of the solar plexus helps to surmount the confusion of the nerve centers; that is why the serpent was a regal symbol. When the coils of the serpent begin to curl, the organism becomes especially sensitive. Flowers transmit their vital emanation through the fibres of the tissues of the white blood corpuscles, which defend the citadel of the serpent. In nature, serpents love flowers; similarly, the serpent of the solar plexus is nourished by them.

El Morya

From the front row of the synagogue where I sat with my friend, the Rabbi looked bigger than life. A big man in his 40s, his presence commanded attention as he came forward to position himself on the *bimah*. Reading from the Torah, his sensitive face and strong, mellifluous voice made this Passover special. It was my first time hearing the epic history of the Jewish people, and in great cadences and solemn vocalizations, his liturgy resounded against the synagogue walls like a 5-part chorus. With his every word unifying the congregation on this most sacred day, the Rabbi administered to us a dose of strong Jewish medicine.

As the Jewish saga unraveled, I began to feel something vaguely familiar. As if a hidden part of me was being explored, I noticed my heart roused at the Rabbi's recounting of the long suffering of his people and the Diaspora. His genuine love of the Holy Land and soulful prayers filled me to such saturation, I was his captive. It was a feeling of rapture much like the overwhelming sensations of a supreme musical score at the supreme moment of a great film. I assumed the entire congregation was experiencing the Rabbi's profundity as we sat in the synagogue on this most important feast day commemorating the exodus of the Jews from Egypt.

During his reading of the Passover Haggadah, a strong thread from the Rabbi's heart conjoined with mine in sympathetic vibration.

The longer he read, the more I entered into the Jewish soul–the psyche of a people; within the hour, uncontrollable tears began streaming down my face. Embarrassed, I excused myself, fearful the impending downpour would interrupt the service. Calming down in the powder room, I returned to my seat, exchanging a feeble glance over to my friend next to me, signaling 'all was well', when in truth, I had little confidence–stuffing my purse full of emergency Kleenex. Within minutes I felt the second outpouring gathering inside, indicating its inexorable force. I quickly excused myself again–this time for good. It was just in time, as the levees now burst anew. Relegated to hearing the liturgy from a safe distance, I positioned myself behind a walled partition, unseen–keeping my eyes trained on the soothing colors of the stained-glass design of *The Lion of Judah*.

On the drive home I was unable to respond coherently to my curious Jewish hosts, apologizing to their daughter for my behavior. So discomforted by the emotional drain, I desperately needed peace. In silence, I turned my attention outside the car window to gather my wits, to ponder on what set off this Passover tsunami. Setting my jaw, I was intent on following the trail of tears to its source.

Recalling that Yiddish was routinely spoken by all my father's siblings set me to wondering. Again. We certainly acted Jewish with all the Yiddish spoken around the home. I had questioned my uncles, my aunt and my father about being Jewish–and each time I was thrown a red herring. Looking out the car window, it all started to gel. I became adamant, determined that I would not be left in the lurch again. I was not going away until I learned the truth. Marching straight into the den with my purse bulging with wet Kleenex, I cornered my father, who immediately sized up the situation from the unusual sight standing before him: His pitiful daughter looked very much the child in distress, eyelids red and swollen, her bearing exasperated.

The next full hour was sobering. I never viewed life quite the same again, most especially the etching – immortalized on my 12-year-old mind – by the transformation that came over father's face as he revealed our Jewish secret. In the blink of an eye, his native, comical spontaneity vanished; taking its place were the terrible truths that obstructed the freedoms of U.S. citizens as well as those around the globe. Feeding me carefully framed phrases–in bite-sized pieces–he began to explain the hidden fears facing the Jews. Doling out mindful rations lest he say too much–handing his thoughts to me as if they contained fragile, precious cargo–he spoke softly, as if someone might be listening.

Someone could have been; his fears were well-founded: We were living in the later years of the Red-Scare, an era of witch hunts. The FBIs' J.Edgar Hoover was keen to burn "witches" while Senator Joseph McCarthy was spreading fear all across the nation. Through power vested by the *House Committee on Un-American Activities*, the government was actively conducting surveillance, wiretapping, incarcerating, character-assassinating and 'Blacklisting' thousands of innocent people–ultimately ruining the lives of anyone suspected of being a Communist threat–or Jewish. Among Hollywood's 'Blacklisted' were prominent figures–including Charlie Chaplin, Woody Guthrie and Pete Seeger–as well as producers, actors, directors and musicians, all of whom they framed as dangerous Communist threats, Jewish ancestry a target. The Communist fear frenzy was raging through the nation–a nation which was not yet recovered from the numbing shock of World War II under Hitler's Nazi Germany.

My father's concerns revolved chiefly around three factors: Our family was both German *and* Jewish. Furthermore my father made his living in the Hollywood music studios, and both his parents had worked in Hollywood as well. According to the midget minds holding the power at the time–all of Hollywood was suspect!

Father's confession to me on that Passover night was a huge life lesson. There was the lesson of causes and their effects; of abuses of power; of the deadly effects of slander and gossip; of how one poisoned mind can contaminate and immobilize a nation; of the necessity for balanced justice; of the crippling tragedy of war; of the psychological scars of national shame; of the urgency for healing relations among all nations...

Two great nations–Germany and the United States–had both quaked, weakened by poisonous ideas focused in the minds of the ignorant few.

Chapter 8   Fourteen Canaries

Comedy often compensates for tragedy, as it did on my father's side of the family. En mass, my paternal uncles spoke nothing if not German-Yiddish dialect, making our house rumble with peals of laughter, one outdoing the other–constantly joking, rhyming and just generally horsing around with the next Yiddish story or limerick. Their peals could be heard from afar. The levity continued on for hours.

One of their favorite jokes was retold often–tweaked with each new version. The story involves a young newlywed Jewess who is being introduced into her new neighborhood of middle-aged, married Jewesses for the first time. During the luncheon, the hostess engages the newlywed in a typical Jewish boast:

Hostess: "Mine Herschel vas givink (giving) to me on my weddink (wedding) day a nize (nice), sowoft (soft), minker (mink) coat dat (that) cost thousands."

First Jewess guest: "Mine Asher vas givink to me on my weddink day a beautiful Lincoln Continental mit (with) all the finest gadgets, and I'm tellink (telling) you it cost plenty."

Second Jewess guest: "Mine Hymen vas givink to me on my weddink day da (the) most beautiful houz (house) in Beverly Hills dat you ever saw."

Third Jewess guest: "Mine Abraham vas givink to me on my weddink day a 40 carat diamond bracelet, I'm tellink you it vas (was) so vunderful (wonderful)."

At this point all the married Jewesses turn to signal the young newlywed Jewish princess. It is her turn to boast of her new husband's economic surplus, but the newlywed Jewess is overcome with shame as she and her new husband are young and have very little money saved. In pure innocence she tells her simple truth:

"Mine David is a good man. Someday he vil (will) buy me all that I esk(ask), just like a good Jewish boy. Ve(We) haf (have) very little money. But I vil (will) be honest—mine David vil (will) someday give us many sons. This I know because mine David vas (was) havink (having[has]) a schmuck (penis) so long...like dis (she demonstrates the size of her husband's penis by extending her arm out to 90°)... a schmuck so long...his schmuck I'm tellink you, dat 14 canaries could schtood" (could stand upon it).

At the newlywed's humble admission, the Jewesses are ridden with guilt. They look at each other in shame for having caused such humiliation to their nice new neighbor. Each in turn seeks favor by paying the necessary reparations:

Hostess: "You know, I vas not tellink the truth ven I said dat mine Herschel vas givink me on my weddink day a nice, sowoft, minker dat cost thousands. The truth is, da fur vas only rabbit!"

First Jewess guest: "I said dat mine Asher vas givink to me on my weddink day a beautiful Lincoln Continental mit all the finest gadgets. Vell, if I'm tellink you da truth, it vas only a Volkswagon!"

Second Jewess guest: " I said mine Hymen vas givink to me on my weddink day da most beautiful houz in Beverly Hills. To be tellink da truth, it vas only a small houz in Bel Air!"

Third Jewess guest: "Mine Abraham I vas tellink you vas givink to me on my weddink day a 40 carat diamond bracelet. I'm tellink you it vas only 5 carats."

Hearing these confessions, the newlywed Jewess now feels filled with remorse, guilty for having overstated her husband's estimable physical gifts. She is likewise compelled to modify her own story, thus:

"I said mine David vas havink a schmuck so long (she again extends her arm out to 90°) dat 14 canaries could schtood. I'm ashamed dat I am not qvite(quite) tellink you da truth" she admits, demonstrating the length of her husband's penis by standing on one foot. "Da truth is not qvite like dat, the last canary...he stands like dis."

Chapter 9   Relocation & Vietnam

I found an island in your arms
Country in your eyes
Arms that chain
Eyes that lie
Break on through to the other side
Break on through to the other side

The Doors, 1967

Pigs also trample upon flowers, but without any effect on themselves.
Therefore, without conscious consumption of the vital emanation one
may pass over the best remedies. Hence the desire to see the flowers
unplucked.

El Morya

The 60s was a fast-forward blur. We moved from Santa Monica to the Pacific Palisades less than 2 years into middle school. Nixon would take the torch from LBJ, escalating the Vietnam war, claiming 1,200 of America's sons each month. Anti-war marches and race riots plastered the front page of the *L.A. Times*. Revolution was in the air. Under the Nixon doctrine, the ocean of the 60s turned ugly, rotten, toxic.

LSD hit the streets. San Francisco flower children–growing little flower children in their bellies–dosed on the streets at Haight-Ashbury. The Beatles and the Doors debuted on Ed Sullivan. *Hair* opened at the Aquarius Theater on Sunset Boulevard in 1968. A mother gave birth to her child on Yasgur's Farm, below the stage where performers like Jimi Hendrix and Janis Joplin rocked the 1969 Woodstock Festival. Music legends would pass from the screen of life before Woodstock reached its second birthday; within one year we would lose Jim Morrison. Janis and Jimmy would follow him.

The politics of deception was sweeping the baby-boomer generation out to sea. An eerie presence was circling around us, unseen–dorsal fins of political sharks moving about in subterfuge. In the cold, dark waters of the times, there were no moorings, no bearings. There was no precedence, no reference. The government's agenda raged on in cold-hearted war-mongering, taking American sons daily to their death. Mothers were self-medicating with valium and alcohol, their sons and daughters overdosing on psychedelics. A dark, heavy mass lingered in the atmosphere, supercharging the heightened tension. The soul of the nation was being altered.

"Something's happening here, what is is ain't exactly clear..." could not have caricatured more consummately the ominous state of the union when *Buffalo Springfield* released those somber words, January, 1967 and *Country Joe and the Fish* sang their famous anti-war mantra: *"Hell no, we won't go"*! Big Brother was everywhere–the unassailable enemy–their deadly fumes permeating deep into the skin of a nation ailing from the stench of war, death and deception. Across the seams, the fabric of a young generation was rent wide–carving indelible scars on the psyche of the age. American society was breaking down.

For the first and only time in my life I argued with my father, a Nixon Republican. At full throttle I pushed on him, insisting that surely he would oppose the war if women were being drafted. I scolded him for denying the facts: he had no sons to lose. His lack of vision alarmed me–I was losing my best friend. Something was indeed "rotten in the state of Denmark" to have addled our relationship. The same viper whose fangs penetrated deep into the nation's soul was now working its venom in less subtle ways, separating inseparable loved ones from each other.

A strange miasma clouded America, feeding on us like threads of parasitic hyphae, depleting the nation's vital essence. The nation's heart was breaking. As these conditions prevailed on the heart of the nation, my own heart would be crushed before I turned 16–sending me headfirst down a rabbit hole into a deep depression.

Chapter 10 Metamorphosis

To everything, turn, turn, turn
There is a season, turn, turn, turn
And a time to every purpose under heaven

Pete Seeger 1959, Adapted from The Book of Ecclesiastes

Our communions reveal the book of the growth of the spirit's
understanding. Not by the way of miracle but by that of daily routine
do We work. I vouch that even from spawn one can learn. Each ovum
of the spawn bears a complete organism. Thus, a many-hued sac of
thought imbues space.

El Morya

The butterfly is a Lepidopterous insect whose life cycle evolves through what entomologists describe as *complete metamorphosis*–emerging from egg to larva to pupa and on to its final destination–the reproductive stage of the adult. From the perspective of the entomologist–if *Homo sapiens* were to be compared with *Lepidopterans*–it could be said that the particular stage of life we humans enter at the time of high school is analogous to the third stage in the life cycle of the Butterfly–the pupa, a teenage butterfly, as it were. Having passed through the larval stage–characterized by the caterpillar's voracious appetite, amassing huge quantities of food for its rapid growth–my body likewise was already slightly swollen in certain areas, in need of support and protection. Similarly, the pupa's encasement–the cocoon–insulates the embryonic butterfly, safeguarding it until emergence, when the adult can fly away from natural predators.

The entomologist speaks of the pupal stage–the chrysalis–as one in which specialized cells prepare the creature living inside for the impending phenomenon–when the shape-shifting chrysalis emerges into the adult butterfly. The "chrysalis" of my young body was likewise busy accommodating signals from my endocrine glands, busy adapting to changes at each menstrual cycle–my teenage body maturing far faster than my brain. Unlike butterflies, *Homo sapiens'* mental processes must undergo much future development before nature's precision ultimately resolves the phenomenon.

I entered high school feeling as a stranger feels: isolated. All around me paraded pupas in butterfly costumes, young females masquerading in a faux mating display, as if they had reached the adult stage. The butterflies competed with each other in their costuming–dressed to impress, obeying some untenable dress code, whose trends–like dogmas–changed to suit the season. I counted myself as an outsider to this time-and-energy consuming pageantry, perplexed by the changing displays. Wading at the waters' edge, I watched in wonder at the scads of high-fashion fish, swishing in their miniskirts and boots–this week imitating the high fashions of *Twiggy*. Sadly, some of the 60s butterflies never did make it to the adult stage, their chrysalis consumed by predators or swallowed up by the strange times. Some would never fly.

Inside my chrysalis, some mystifying energy was calling me urgently into a ritual dance, in step with my hormonal rushings: Nature was celebrating my arrival. On the other hand, conflicting signals entered into the mix: The committee supervisors–those for my head, body and heart–did not always agree, at times running amok. I suppose I could say I wallowed somewhat in a conflict of interests. The young brain on my head was unfit to be captain at this passage through the wild seas of youth in the 60s. Our whole generation was out to sea, well beyond the *Arc of Visibility*–where the horizon can no longer be sighted and navigation is uncertain. My instincts gave me ample warning that my vessel would become unseaworthy were I to follow the fish pooling around me–some swimming many leagues into uncharted waters, some consumed by the snares of Neptune's left-handed delusions. I tried my best to calculate to true north the bearings of my own compass. I thought of myself as impenetrable–which sentiment was confirmed more than a few times. My father's words of wisdom had alerted me to the perils on the open sea, where many a tempest throws many a traveler overboard. I always believed I could navigate as well as a pelagic bird; I had a strong internal guidance system.

Chapter 11   Chinese Noodle

As I walked out, felt my own need just beginning
I'll wait in the queue when the trains come back
Lie with you where the shadows run from themselves

Cream, 1968

Joe entered my life my sixteenth summer. Invited to a party, I called upon my boy-crazy friend, Robin, from the old neighborhood–ever the willing party chauffeur. Scanning the radio stations en route I tuned in to the perfect party primer. Joining us in song was Jim Morrison, belting out *"Light my Fire"*. Still flower crazy, the sight of gorgeous *Erythrina caffra* trees in full coral bloom made the drive along San Vicente Boulevard a glorious one, raising my spirits high. Euphoric, we sang songs all the way from the Pacific Palisades to Brentwood–our destination.

The welcoming sound of live British music coming from the party house had me skipping up the stairs, two-at-a-time. Once inside, my body was seized on contact from the throbbing rhythms of *Fresh Cream's* latest release. The sheer power of the sound stirred everyone in the crowd, making my own venous blood instantly heat up to simmering. With Robin-bird in tow, the two of us passed through the long hallway to a room swelling with clusters of uninhibited dancers aroused by the rich sounds saturating the atmosphere. When the music stopped the excited throng relaxed somewhat, making the wild banshees appear more like clusters of sea anemones flailing their arms more slowly–giving us a chance to burrow an aisle through the sea of dancers without getting slapped.

We made our way to the large ballroom area at the moment the band's next song ripped through the loud speakers. Apprehending my heart was the commanding urgency of *White Room*–thrilling in its complex timing changes, hauntingly beautiful in its vocal intensity. My ear took in the sound as if it were a miracle; I was not alone. Landing on American shores during the 60s', rock groups from England, the"British Invasion," entered our country just in time to invigorate our souls, to clear the stultifying chaos of the Nixon years.

The sheer power of the live guitar rhythms pursued me with authority, beckoning me—and at the same time—liberating me. I danced unabashedly, spinning like a whirligig—my eyes shut, lead by one thought alone: I must follow this sound and express myself through dance, for dancing to this music sustains my soul in a way that no other art has ever been able to do.

Swirling past huddles of smoking heads, dancing my heart out as I approached the stage—someone caught my arm with strong determination, as if to take possession of me. I gave a quick smile in response, breaking free from his grip with another twirl. I was in a state of profound inspiration, fixed solely on expressing love for this gorgeous music. There is an undeniable freeing action I find only through dance and I was not about to relinquish that freedom so easily. Unfazed, I returned to my higher purpose, moving unrestricted across the room, whizzing and whirling as Robin, my loyal companion, followed after me—watching the petite dancer clad in a lipstick-pink miniskirt—her long, blond hair shimmering under the strobe lights, flowing as free as wind across wild oats.

At session break, the lead singer/ rhythm guitarist found me outside alone, breathing the sweet orange-blossom fragrance of *Pittosporum undulatum* trees that so often perfume California nights. Setting his face squarely upon mine, he took my hand gently. I saw at once he had come for some serious business and I flinched repeatedly, vacillating between his advances. He was getting to know me too quickly. I retreated into shy mode but he maneuvered adroitly, giving me the impression he was not about to lose this round. Following the shoals and rocky outcroppings of my edgy hesitance—he came clear up to the border of my autonomous region and instinctively knew to back up a bit—sensing my flight response. Probing more gently and with very sweet words, he took my hand again, trying to get me to move closer to him.

At first, my fifteen+ years of leonine pride held sway, denying him a passport to enter my native habitat. I felt somewhat afraid of him, yet allured. When my protectoress instincts called me back to safety is when he maneuvered–equal to the challenge–almost as if he could read me. He could. Swift as a falconer, the knight in all his appurtenances alighted on the promontory of the damsel's fortified citadel, presenting himself nobly in the pursuit of the protesting lass. Imploring his damsel to await his pleasure–he would be at his lady's service within the hour.

How could I resist the dark-eyed beauty entreating me with such rare charm? Not many could. Never mind that his smile could light up a room. This Italian cross breed with ivory skin–so dashing in his British mutton chops and shiny dark hair that touched down to his shoulders–also came equipped with a honeycomb voice that could thaw the Greenland ice sheet. This very shiny copper penny was insistent that I wait for him. He *really* wanted to see me again and I was–in spite of all my leonine protesting–genuinely flattered.

This was how I met Joe: the Mass-saying, good Roman Catholic boy–the 19 year old Italian who would sweep me off my feet. Had I found my Catholic mensch? Was I headed toward the promised land? Not exactly... This is the one guy who would lift my virgin soul to Olympian heights–heights from which I would fall, crash and burn–leaving ashes of a scrambled mainframe, my CPU dangling in unreadable machine language.

Naïve in the boyfriend area, I was a virgin blossom still blushing from male advances, keeping a safe distance. I trusted only one man–my hero father, my idol. Boys told me in later years they were afraid to so much as advance a hand towards me. Not so Joe! The charming knight took total command of his young charge, handling with care the unwrapped package of my fragile youth. Walking with his arm wrapped around me, I felt as if I were embraced by a warm, tropical rain belt.

Was it his music that sent my spirit flying over the rainbow? Was it *Romeo* who stood on stage singing *Sunshine of Your Love* to his *Juliet*–

addressing me across a capacity crowd, singing: *"I've been waiting so long"*? Was it his beauty? What was it that sent unchecked electricity coursing through my young body? The knight's charms had turned the lioness inside-out. Milliards of neuron fibers sent my vagus nerve into overtime as sensory ganglia signaled early warning signs of a love tsunami. Under the influence of his manifold charms, I was wobbling like a Chinese noodle.

Chapter 12   Song of Solomon

I adjure you, O daughters of Jerusalem,
by the gazelles, and by the hinds of the field,
that ye awaken not, nor stir up love, until it please.

Song of Solomon, Jewish Publication Society 1917

...One balmy afternoon in rutting season during the autumn equinox,
the hart and his young doe went out to graze the green fields upon the
hills of En-geddi...

It was a Sunday date. As we drove southward along the peridot-green Pacific, I followed the endless cycles of waves–mounting up into sweeping crests and crashing down with powerful Neptunian authority, ejecting their silvery-white dew onto the glistening sand. Our four mile drive–from my parents' house to the Santa Monica onramp–was punctuated by heavy kissing at every pause in heavy traffic. He was a superb kisser and I responded eagerly to his young manhood, stimulated by the Italian seasoning of the natural musk emanating from his perfect skin.

Ascending the Santa Monica ramp, it was not long before he pulled into the driveway of his British pal, who had kindly offered up his flat for the afternoon. Leading me inside by the hand and shutting the door behind him, Joe pulled me in very tight, kissing me as we stood just inside the threshold. Taking my hand, he led me over to the stereo system, selected from a library of LPs, and set a stack on the turntable, adjusting the volume controls–bringing me in close, just as the music began to play. Straightaway the room was suffused with a breathing, vital essence–saturating everything within the walls–the room syncopated in a seductive throbbing.

Bringing my face just inches from his–Joe stood for a long moment searching my eyes. Releasing an ecstatic moan, he launched his lips upon mine—putting to sea a mighty love boat down the slipway of my mouth. Calling out my name between kisses, his honey-voice anointed our union. He made humming sounds like an Italian drone bee, helpless to do other than worship and mate with his queen. My own passions were cycling higher and higher in the bliss, accelerating his desire. Our mutual delight, communicating its own language of our hunger, was worthy of a beautiful poem.

Slowly, with our bodies bonded, he led me over to the couch. Setting me down gently on soft cushions, he took my chin in his hands like a cup—caressing my face, speaking in whispers of his desire. Oh, those brown eyes of his, they sparkle like diamonds. Reading his face was a page turner of delightful moment: rich in treasure, paradise found. Kissing me deeply again, it was not long before we were cooking up some pretty good thermals. With his mouth locked onto mine, his hands began to trace gently my body, mapping it sweetly at first—and then more thoroughly—almost every inch of my world. Pulling his lips from mine, his lips now desired to follow his hands, sweetly kissing and caressing the topography. Moaning, circling my breasts, he lost his breath. Returning to my face—calling my name, his kisses came at me again and again.

A salty drop of dew from his face lingered on my lips, mingling with the aromatic musk now pouring out his skin. His fragrance reached into my nostrils, causing giant waves of arousal to erupt in undulations through my body—signaling in secretions of my desire—unlocking my heart from captivity, overwhelming me. Recovering momentarily from the heights of ecstasy, at the very moment I took in air to ease my quivering—my lover found a secret spot on my neck—sending me careening like a shooting star.

The more courageous his hands, the higher my body climbed in ecstasy....each plateau higher with each thrust of his fingers, gliding through the moist lubrications of my harbor. Maintaining his course, my Master took full control of my body, which I gave over to him willingly. Obedient to his urgency, the sheer power of our fleshly union lulled me into its portal: Submitting to the force of erotica, I was absorbed into it, leaving my body–no longer earthly–but lightly tethered to a new paradise of otherworldly pleasures...

...I am an instrument in my King's hands. He strums melodies of sweetness upon my body, which is his love harp. My King rejoices at the trembling of my strings as we glide through a ceaseless eternity of giving and receiving. My beloved King encloses me now, as within an iridescence of pastel petals...a blossom of surpassing beauty now coalescing, now becoming... I AM become his beautiful flower...

I am a rose of Sharon, a lily of the valleys,

As a lily among thorns, so is my love among the daughters.

He hath brought me to the banqueting-house, and his banner over me is love.

Let his left hand be under my head, and his right hand embraces me.

'I adjure you, O daughters of Jerusalem, by the gazelles, and by the hinds of the field, that ye awaken not, nor stir up love, until it please.'

Behold, thou art fair, my love; behold, thou art fair; thine eyes are as doves behind thy veil; thy hair is as a flock of goats, that trail down from mount Gilead.

Thy two breasts are like two fawns that are twins of a gazelle, which feed among the lilies.

Thy lips, O my bride, drop honey--honey and milk are under thy tongue; and the smell of thy garments is like the smell of Lebanon.

Thou art a fountain of gardens, a well of living waters, and flowing streams from Lebanon.

Awake, O north wind; and come, thou south; blow upon my garden, that the spices thereof may flow out. Let my beloved come into his garden, and eat his precious fruits.

I said: 'I will climb up into the palm-tree, I will take hold of the branches thereof; and let thy breasts be as clusters of the vine, and the smell of thy countenance like apples;

And the roof of thy mouth like the best wine, that glideth down smoothly for my beloved, moving gently the lips of those that are asleep.' I am my beloved's, and his desire is toward me.

'I adjure you, O daughters of Jerusalem, by the gazelles, and by the hinds of the field, that ye awaken not, nor stir up love, until it please.'

Make haste, my beloved, and be thou like to a gazelle or to a young hart upon the mountains of spices.

Chapter 13   Sorrento Playboy

In the chilly hours and minutes of uncertainty
I want to be
In the warm hold of your loving mind
To feel you all around me and to take your hand
Along the sand
Ah, but I may as well try and catch the wind

Donovan Leitch, 1965

Opening my eyes I beheld my King Solomon: His left hand roamed his lady's belly while his right hand parted her thighs–toward which his lips were making their merry way. Moaning in the heat of his passion, his mouth came upon the chaste walls of the virgin palace, his tongue moving over the golden gates which glistened before her temple. She beheld her King–kneeling in genuflection–before entering into her holy place, desirous of worshipping at her sacred fountain.

Returning to its seat upon her crown, her rational brain began to register a vague confirmation of a return from the fastnesses of space. Now seeing her body on the couch where she had left it, she was only half-way back in her body.

The first warning signal alighted subtly–impressing her with a delicate suggestion that perhaps the royal couple might stop their delicious feasting now before losing complete control of their royal appetites. She denied the thought; she could not bear to leave the worshipping Solomon.

The second warning was less subtle. She sensed a presence of foreboding when a messenger conveyed a sign–presenting an image of a bird which hovered over the couch, circling the pair writhing in a euphoric state–but which had not coupled to completion.

Enter the large bird–the size of a stork–carrying a wrapped bundle in its mouth. I woke up! Electrified! The message surged clear through me, petrifying me as a mute stone, then jolting me back into sinus rhythm. The symbolism was clear, a vision of substance: 'This far and no farther'. Reacting in haste, I panicked, clumsily gathering together the still-floating fragments of myself, commanding full cohesion of my body and mind. Removing in sudden retreat–I could not speak. I could not think. I could only look down at the beautiful youth I had cast off so unmercifully. A pitiful sight it was to see Joe as he remained motionless–still anchored in genuflection.

My starry-eyed expedition had indeed landed abruptly. Only at the final sidereal crossing was I saved–by a return current of energy blocking my flight pattern, signaling me back from space by a divine travelers' alert warning me of the dangers of oxygen deprivation at higher altitudes. Clearly an amateur pilot, my brain was no guide at those heights which tend to bend the rational mind. I should *not* have been flying into space *and* romancing at the same time. I confess: I was winging my way in space while under the influence of *Eros*–flying far beyond the safe speed limit. Endorphin overdose. I am forever grateful for that divine intercession; my fealty is sworn to the avian officer who signaled me to buckle up and head home.

Our next communication was Joe's Hallmark card, arriving in my mailbox several months later, half-heartedly suggesting a reunion. Ha! It was way too late for that. My vanity had been sequestered; protected now by walls built thicker with each day that his call did not come.

I cast myself in a starring role in my own drama. Ever the tragic heroine–picking up the leftover scraps of my self esteem–I locked myself away in my bedroom, poring over his photograph. Writing day after day in the madness of a poet, tears stained the pages of my lovelorn poetry. My Roman Catholic Messiah had shattered my dreams. In useless self-pity, I was the self-mortifying nun in her lonely cell, the self-flagellating martyr in her self-made sarcophagus. Intent on denying all future carnal pleasure–pleasure which I linked, inextricably, with severe anguish and pain–I just wanted to be left alone with my poetry and its muse–Joe's photograph. I was one pathetic case.

The truth always comes out and when it did, the tone of my poems changed: When my good Catholic boy was seen trolling Sorrento Beach–a fashionable volleyball meat market–casting a wide net for colorful Santa Monica fish, that signaled the end of the good ship. That painful information was quite enough to bring out the evil in me–smirking at the thought that at least I had inflicted *some* physical pain on him at our "last supper": My parting gift to him was that I had left him with a majorly blood-swollen set of blue balls. In this new light of truth I quipped:

The Sorrento playboy is back'n
Men try but they ain't got the knack'n
Though none of my biz
Some Playboy he is:
What he needs is a really good whack'n!

Chapter 14   Bruce Juice

The greatness of Cosmos precludes scrutiny; it overwhelms and exalts.
Spirit-knowledge is cognized by the spirit's knowledge. Pay attention
to the silvery thread that connects one in spirit with the spirit of the
Guide and extends its silvery manifestation up to the Ruler of the
Planet. There results a network of conduits from the Supreme Spirit.

El Morya

Seven years. That's how long before I could unthaw the goods in my freezer. The math was simple: Eros equals crucifixion. I had fallen at the third station and didn't want to try it again. No one was going to tamper with the goods.

I developed an affinity with fast cars. I had no fear in Don's 1960s Roadster Porsche, screeching around sharp corners in Topanga Canyon, and bouncing through high water on Malibu Creek Road in Steve's Land Rover. With the wind in my hair, I began to taste my lost freedom. Returning home, I continued my isolation, writing.

My parents checked for vital signs, deciding to put me in a private school. My father had little faith in teenage self-control, concerned from all the male attention I was getting–made patently clear from his string of friendly reminders: "Juee, if you ever get pregnant, you can always tell me and I'll take you to Europe." Abortions in the 60s were illegal in America and those that were performed underground, well–you really don't want to know.

Some time near graduation, eight of us packed into a van to the San Francisco Fillmore West–Jethro Tull opened for Led Zeppelin. After that experience, I gave up all synthetic highs to posterity. With my bird-like constitution, I didn't need any help getting airborne. So it came as somewhat of a shock when my father asked me for some marijuana.

My open-minded father, always the rational scientist–wanted to experience what it was like to get high. A teetotaler, running 3-5 miles per day and following a strict regimen of healthy eating–suddenly my Dad decides to experiment with the herb! His longtime musician friend offered to sponsor his experiment. After smoking several joints at Desi's pot party, my father could perceive no change whatsoever in his mental processes. The test having failed, the scientist decides on further testing, whereupon a bulging bag of Desi's pot came home with the scientist, for testing in his own laboratory.

I knew nothing of his plan. One weekend, when my mother happened to be a safe distance away from home, I saw my father open the sliding glass door–about to enter the kitchen–and stop in mid-step. It was a curious sight to watch him trying to maneuver through the door, burdened as he was–holding several 2 x 12-foot-long boards of lumber. Mentally concentrated, he tried his best to measure by visual calculations–gauging whether the space would allow for the passage of his cargo without breaking the glass door or scratching the kitchen table which barred his path.

"Dad! What *are* you doing?" I asked, in wonderment. Halting in self-examination, he looked at the lumber in his arms–seizing up in voluminous laughter. "I don't know, Juee. What the hell *am* I doing?" He surrendered–no contest, guilty as charged. Sizing up the situation, I ordered my father–under no condition–to answer the phone until he came down from his high, suggesting bed rest. But first I wanted the whole story.

"Well, Juee, Desi gave me some marijuana to try, but after an hour I still could not feel a damn thing. His friends were smoking and laughing, but I didn't see what was so funny. I told Desi the marijuana must not be very strong. So Desi gave me a bag of it to take home and warned me, 'Bruce, *do not* smoke this all at once, it is *sinsemilla*–very potent stuff.' So, this morning, I did the same as I do with my *Greeners*: I put the whole bag into the blender with water, strained the juice–then down the hatch. You know...it gave me a bad case of the runs—has a strong laxative effect. I had to visit the crapper all day long. That's where I was headed when you saw me coming into the kitchen."

Chapter 15   Brazilian Orchids

According to the color of his radiation, each one is attracted by flowers. White and lilac have affinity with the purple, blue with the blue; therefore, I advise to keep more of these colors in the room. One can follow this in living flowers. Plants wisely selected according to color are more healing. I advise to have more freesias. Our Ray, with its silveriness, is more reminiscent of white flowers. Color and sound are Our best repast.

El Morya

At a rolling Pacific Palisades estate, I began a weekend job–my first real job–training under an orchid enthusiast. George's prized collection of Brazilian orchids was already immense and growing larger each year. A shipment had just arrived, which had kept him waiting months before passing through USDA quarantine inspection. My first day at work George was in a state of high anxiety–simultaneously excited *and* irritable. Any small deviation that interrupted his greenhouse work intensified his angst. His nervous tension had valid origins, considering the time, cost and fragile nature of his imports–but his plans seemed to vacillate, minute-by-minute.

Under his ever-watchful eye, I apprenticed in the art of precision transplanting, setting tiny terrestrial orchid seedlings into George's specially blended medium: fir bark, peat moss, and Osmunda fiber. His mantra, warning me to use gentle hands, was not so gentle–castigating me, repeating that these imports would be at least three–possibly as many as eight years–before blooming.

Each weekend I believed I was being fired. George would get furious with me, claiming I was rushing, changing the next moment–correcting my work as being too slow–the fragile imports at risk of drying out. Pushing me to the brink more than a few times, George offered me another aptitude test: keeping cool under constant fire. Having had early training by my sisters, I was already versed in deep breathing to maintain composure–but each Sunday afternoon when the day was done, I left work feeling totally ransacked.

George would make annoying *clucking* sounds when he was hyper– and since he was always hyper, every Sunday with George was like working in a henhouse. He had the habit of pacing up and down his greenhouse rows, incessantly monitoring the health of his costly specimens, fussing like a gravid laying hen. Dutifully echoing him in perfect mimicry was his Amazon parrot–the two of them bouncing off each other in annoying, piercing syncopation. Such was the vocal bond between man and bird. Second-in-command of his masters' estate, that bird went everywhere George went, squawking from atop the numerous, custom-made bird stands, ubiquitously located throughout the estate. The Amazon's bill being good for about 1500 psi, I was careful to maintain a safe distance passing by the avian screamer.

Under the tutelage of the ultra-sensitive, lisping perfectionist, it was a miracle that George kept me employed through the 2-month project. Immunizing myself from the obnoxious tension in the greenhouses, I kept riveted on the business at hand. Hot as a laser beam, the heat of George's angst braised me from long distance, searing my ear canals with volatile directives. Standing over me like a *Hovercraft*, his hot breath clinging to my cheek–my apprentice fingers trembled as I removed from a tiny flask–ever so gingerly– imported mericlones of *Cattleya leopoldii*.

To be fair, George's tempest did turn calm when he spoke of *leopoldii's* nativity–coming as it did from a swamp in the coastal plains just above Espírito Santo, Brazil; and of how the mericlones required many months' growth in a gelatinous agar solution before the first tiny leaves would emerge. Partial to his *Catasetum spitzii* orchids, he got excited telling me they were collected in their typical habitat, growing on mature *Tabebuia* trees. I happened to be in love with *Tabebuia*, making regular visits to the gorgeous yellow flowering specimen on Sunset Boulevard, one block from the coast.

The day I crossed the orchid transplanting finish line, I took the final breath, vowing to avoid such work in the future; I had discovered my tolerance threshold for delicate manual precision. I did carry away with me forever a great gift, however: the olfactory memory of greenhouse orchids. Closing my eyes today–when I fix the image of Brazilian Cattleyas, my nose bulbs swiftly link up– *toute suite!* The exotic memory of orchid perfume emanating from a greenhouse is as real as if I were holding a flower up to my nostrils. If I needed a beauty muse, now I could count on Brazilian orchids.

Chapter 16   Topanga Canyon

TARLETON. All this damned materialism: what good is it to anybody? I've got a soul: don't tell me I haven't. Cut me up and you can't find it. Cut up a steam engine and you can't find the steam. But, by George, it makes the engine go. Say what you will, Summerhays, the divine spark is a fact.

LORD SUMMERHAYS: Have I denied it?

TARLETON. Our whole civilization is a denial of it. Read Walt Whitman.

George Bernard Shaw, Misalliance 1909

My father had bought me the safest vehicle on the market. Turning my silver Ford Falcon off the Pacific Coast Highway onto Topanga Canyon to the Malibu Feed Bin for a bale of alfalfa, I pulled into the driveway next door with the goods for my horse. A young mother at eighteen, my sister–third in the sibling line–plus her toddler daughter shared the house with me, one of the very few such houses at the immediate crossroads. Rentals were rare in the southernmost reaches of Malibu; the waiting list for beach rentals had for years been growing and by the early 70s a long and pushy queue of surfers demanded their due. Obtaining such a rental was part luck, part timing–plus you absolutely needed an agent who could get the job done. My sister's friend ran quarterback for us, winning the day–negotiating boldly with the landowner, intervening on our behalf through the obfuscations of the messy business.

Across the coast highway from our house stretched a strand of beach where, back then, I rode my quarter horse "Kitty"–splashing miles of salty foam in our wild, galloping days–bareback and barefooted. Until my friend returned from U.C.Berkeley and reclaimed *Kitty* a couple years later, the 16-hand buckskin was my dream-horse-come-true. Climbing the trail above the *Rodeo Grounds*, we squeezed through thickets of Chemise and Black Sage, the chaparral playing hide-and-seek on our flanks. Pacing inland along the Topanga Creek watershed, passing a Sycamore tree and the occasional Mountain Mahogany–in winter, singing frogs jumped at our gait. The smell of their damp, leafy habitat lives on in my sound-smell-link memory. A thick wall of invasive Giant Bamboo marked our destination, the limit of *Rodeo Grounds Lane*–where lived my producer-friend, Skip. Kitty and I loved our visits with Skip, our handsome, blonde 40-something friend, whose engaging smile and hilarious personal adventure stories made him a very special treat. He had his own horses so Kitty could always expect some molasses-soaked oats. It was a very sad day when Kitty and I rode up the *Rodeo Grounds* to find Skip losing his hair and his balance, barely making his way to the door to greet us–the only thing still living was his smile. The smile is what I will always remember. Skip was the first friend I lost to AIDS.

When my sister relocated with her daughter to San Diego, I took over her weekend job as EKG technician at St.John's, Santa Monica–where my Mother gave birth to all four of us. I laugh, recalling the day I brazenly alerted a very serious intern who had entered the elevator with me–telling the doc his zipper was down. This doc was very smart, very Jewish and very shy; I used to look for him on my weekend rounds. Finding the two of us alone on the elevator, I grabbed my chance. True gentleman that he was, he reacted in horror, searching frantically–front-side-back-front-side-back, until I mentioned, mercifully, that it was April Fool's Day. This doc happened to be the house intern my very first hour of job training with my sister, who responded, along with us–to the 6:30a.m. *Code Blue alarm*. Awakened from sleep by the emergency, the doc arrived at the room looking so sweet: his uncombed, wiry hair so very *Einsteinian*. Of course, he never knew I existed through my two-years at the hospital, so imagine my luck running into him again–almost 20 years later at a northern California CMA convention (where I was working hospitality)–socializing among his peers during a conference break. Cordially excusing my intrusion, I remarked that we had met a long time back when he was an intern at St. John's. Incredulous, he swiped his doctor friend away, guiding the two of us into semi-privacy where I related the historic April Fools Day zipper caper. I was only looking to share the levity, but we ended up sharing a few dates as well.

It was always April in our house when I was growing up. Coming from a lineage of actors and writers, it became apparent that drama was in my blood too. For a lark, my last year at junior college, I auditioned for George Bernard Shaw's *Misalliance*, winning the part of Lina Szczepanowska, a Polish trapeze artist who enters the stage dressed as an aviatrix–in high boots, goggles and flying jacket– exemplifying the Shavian ideal woman of the early 20th century Britain: libertine, man's equal partner. Mindless at the time to the similarity in both our characters, I just liked playing the character. Already equipped with the costume–I wore my own English riding boots and jodhpurs. It felt completely natural to act the part of Szczepanowska with lines like:

'I am strong. I am skillful. I am brave. I am independent. I am unbought... he dares to ask me to come live with him in this rrrrrrabbit hutch, and take my bread from his hand, and ask him for pocket money, and wear soft clothes, and be his woman! Sooner than that I would stoop to the lowest depths of my profession...'

In retrospect, playing Lina was a perfect fit. I was just like her: sassy, bold, spontaneous–ready and willing to stand up to injustices, undaunted by forces more powerful than myself.

Chapter 17   Yogananda

Meditation
means to remember
that one is not a mortal body
but an immortal soul,
one with God.

Paramahansa Yogananda

I traded my hospital gig for weekends at Sawyer's Nursery on Sunset Boulevard, one block inland from the ocean. My second mentor—after my father, of course—was the wonderful owner, Maurice, who trained me in all things horticultural. First, he tried me out as manager over his mainstay Hispanic landscape crew. The crew, being many heads and many shoulders above my budding horticultural experience—their knowing smiles presaged my early transition back to the nursery center where I belonged. Maurice next had me driving the company van south to a Lawndale greenhouse operation where I delighted in hand-picking plants for the nursery. From terrarium size to 20-inch specimens, I loved filling the van to maximum, smiling all the way home—my aromatic passengers making up for the tangles on the L.A. freeways. I spent my breaks under the shade of Maurice's amazing *Tipuana Tipu* specimen tree. It was hard to pull myself away from the glorious profusion of its bright yellow flowers. Reaching in my lunch bag, I collected *Tipuana* pods, souvenir reminders of the Leguminoseae, the world's third largest plant family after orchids and grasses.

I began crossing Sunset Boulevard to visit the lush, ten-acre *Lake Shrine* Temple grounds across from the nursery. Founded by Swami Paramahansa Yogananda, the botanical grounds embracing the lake had grown into a miracle garden, a verdant palace of fine art. Walking among the grounds, it is impossible not to be calmed by the serene currents flowing through the gardens. The sound of falling water and the perfectly kept flowerbeds instantly makes peace with the senses. Sweet smelling incense floating in the air guides the visitor towards the gift shop and museum, where Yogananda's clothes and musical instruments, lovely gemstones and writings are among the historical pieces on display. Continuing along a verdant greensward one approaches the World Peace Memorial, where a portion of Mahatma Gandhi's ashes are encased in an ancient Chinese sarcophagus. Flanking the sculptured stone are statues of Kuan Shih Yin, the bodhisattva of compassion, whose name translates as "Observing the sounds of the world".

Present everywhere is a tangible sense of world fellowship and peace, accentuated powerfully by the Court of Religions–a symbol unifying the five principal world religions: Christianity, Judaism, Buddhism, Islam, and Hinduism. A statue of Jesus adorns the crest of a waterfall feeding Lake Shrine, home to a pair of swans. Known as *Self Realization Fellowship, SRF*, the gardens became my second home.

Yogananda's life story, *Autobiography of a Yogi*, was a page-turner that reads more like a mystery novel. Because of the similarity to my own visions and echoes, I was eager to saturate myself with his life story. March 7, 1952 is noted by an extraordinary phenomenon: A notarized statement signed by the Director of Forest Lawn Memorial-Park testified: "No physical disintegration was visible in his body even twenty days after death...This state of perfect preservation of a body is, so far as we know from mortuary annals, an unparalleled one... Yogananda's body was apparently in a phenomenal state of immutability."

I was particularly drawn to Yogananda's stern, disciplinarian guru, Sri Yukteswar, who reminded me of my own father. Signing up for the Kriya Yoga Lessons, mailed to students every two weeks, I began to practice meditation. Just as it claims, I found it was so: Using the breath–life force of prana–and concentrated attention and intention, 'Kriya Yoga purifies and strengthens the entire body–part by part–systematically. Eliminating stress, the meditator enters a calm, interiorized state of awareness, enabling the latent powers of concentration to begin their development, expanding the awareness beyond the limitations of body and mind to the interior realization of the meditator's infinite potential'.

The ancient sages, or *rishis* of India observed, during *pranayama* breathing exercises, the revitalization of the life current in the spine and brain as it flows through the cerebrospinal centers, the *chakras*. The ancients found that by revolving the life current continuously up and down the spine through Kriya Yoga, the practitioner's spiritual evolution could be greatly accelerated, their life prolonged. It took me several years of regular Kriya practice before I could maintain deep states of meditation for long periods of time. Gauging from personal inquiries, everyone seems to have different experiences. That said, no one who correctly follows the course outlined by Yogananda ever comes away empty: Inner peace develops quickly; calming sounds become commonplace; a positive outlook on life becomes immediately apparent.

Through continued Kriya practice, in later years I would regularly see in the center of my vision–a pastel-pink tunnel forming at each session–a diaphanous, breathing, pink tunnel, expanding and contracting in a rhythmic bellowing. During one morning meditation in the veteran years, I experienced a tremendous surge of love: Originating in my heart, a nucleus of love throbbed waves of bliss, spreading from my heart outwards in all directions. It was like suddenly striking an aquifer of spring water deep in the ground. Or like an electronic sparkler on the Fourth of July, the heart *sparklies* came coursing all the way to my fingertips and toes, vivifying my entire body.

I noticed a striking similarity between these *Kriya* fireworks and the ecstasies I had with my *Catholic Solomon*–back when Eros sent me flying. Physical orgasms are soon finished-poof! but Kriya meditation ecstasies have long-lasting effects, which build into even longer periods of bliss with continued practice. For me, Kriya seemed to balance my body and mind, effecting a perfect fulcrum–

giving the sensation of a loving spirit caressing me. In time, when my meditations went really deep–*Wow!*–the heart-centered bliss lingered on and on and on, making Kriya almost magical.

Being a product of a scientific father–inculcated as I was in the virtues of double-blind laboratory testing–when my *Kriya* test results continued to repeat the same results, I could conclude a definite hypothesis: Kriya works! Not only did it work, but *Kriya* was proving to be quite the interesting experience. My so-called "atheist" father–while never criticizing Kriya–adroitly passed over my invitations to discuss meditation. Ironically, I see now he already practiced his own kind of contemplations, and that his *avant garde* ideas and inventions must have come to him from the clear light of those contemplations. Always thinking, always reflecting, it was his natural habitat to live life within the laboratory of his thoughts.

Penetrating deeply his own thoughts, my father would voice serious objections to so-called "expert" opinions. Listening carefully, considering the thought processes of the speaker, he always weighed the idea in his own laboratory, to test whether the claim was plausible. Constantly exercising his rational mind, he had built a strong foundational basis from which to judge the worthiness of ideas. With his extraordinary ability to penetrate deeply into complex subjects, he could find the weak link in the chain. Never interrupting a guest with his faulty logic, he gave nothing but a tender, knowing smile. Later he quietly cautioned me, saying "Juee, B.S., total B.S." I would have to aver that he was a bonified *Master B.S. Detector*–nothing but the truth could make it past the sharp prism of his analytical mind.

Through the years my father would surrender to only one philosopher's wisdom alone–that of Jiddu Krishnamurti, who spoke with great precision of the subtleties of the human mind, and challenged scientists and psychologists on their theories. Like my father, Krishnamurti had similar key attributes: A deep respect for nature; he spoke only from personal insights; he belonged to no religious organization; nor did he subscribe to any school of political or ideological thought. Both of them agreed that belief systems, at variance with one another, were the cause of war. My father was glad to find in Krishnamurti a fellow sage who he said: "never once spoke of God."

I understood somewhat why my father declined to so much as pronounce the word "God": So diluted and mangled by abuse, the word had begun to take on the patina of a worn out Las Vegas coin. What rational, sentient being would want to associate himself with the religious swindlers of the day–the ubiquitous television Christian evangelists *diving for dollars* in the pool of their God-fearing faithful, while living a secret life of depravity offstage?

There were certain areas that were off-limits to my guru-father that either he could not or would not discuss. My *otherworldly* questions were just plain uncomfortable for the lovable "atheist" to deal with. Most likely it was *because* my father espoused atheism, that pushed me to get at the perfect truth; to know for certain the existence or the non-existence of a higher intelligence. My father's ardent disbelief in "God" gave me ample fire to rebel *with* a cause, the border separating us I believed to be simply a problem of semantics. At the time, my "God" was simply the highest teacher living within me, my true Self. Were it not for the limited playing field of my puny lexicon back then, I have the sense my father might have been able to follow my thoughts.

It was Yogananda's *Kriya* take-home lessons that saved the day, that years later finally brought the truth home, but it took years to learn to remain in perfect stillness first. Patience–waiting for the whole enchilada to surface–was excruciating long: my spiritual resources were nascent, not yet within reach. The Lotus would not fully emerge above the muddy pond until the detritus of many life lessons no longer blocked my emergence above the surface waters.

Chapter 18   Two Fiddlers

Very ancient mysteries said: "The lingam is the vessel of wisdom," but in time this knowledge was converted into hideous phallic cults, and religion began to prohibit something without knowing exactly why. Whereas, it should have been said simply that the fact of conception is so wondrous that it is impossible to deal with it by ordinary measures.

El Morya

My dream job at the Los Angeles County Arboretum came to an abrupt halt. Prop 13 passed, the Jarvis-Gann initiative wiping out 15% of the workforce, cutting short my first exposure to horticultural research. Testing natural latex production of *Guayule sp.*, my humble responsibilities included micrometer readings and greenhouse culture of untold numbers of *Guayule* cuttings. The research had previously been interrupted during the Nazi scare in the 40s, burning field tests back then, saving their secrets for a future day. At the time, Goodrich tire products were produced exclusively from *Hevea braziliensis,* a tree from the tropical rain forest. Nowadays, the research had moved to becoming more environmentally correct, focusing on sustainable crops, such as the *Guayule* shrub, a native of arid desert regions. On the slow days, I assisted a TMV (tobacco mosaic virus) study, inoculating cucurbit cotyledons with TMV and sterilizing soil in the autoclaves. Among a gazillion commuters, the long commute on the diamond lane–from Malibu to Arcadia–seemed a small sacrifice for what I relished as a dream experience.

Policy wonks prevailed again, shaving off my next part-time position one year after I took the position. *Vocational Horticultural Assistant* was my official title, but I was the only one doing any teaching. Hoping to infuse student interest in the *key of green* I loved so well, there were a dozen such teens ripe to learn. Coaching the group of Hispanic high schoolers for FFA regional competitions, the morning of the meet I lost hope when my most promising student showed up at 6am in sunglasses, reeking of marijuana. Our team received a third place trophy. Back at the high school, the horticulture "teacher" quickly claimed the trophy, taking the award home with him!

That jackass not only taught the kids zero horticulture, he spent class time telling filthy jokes targeted at women's anatomical parts. Incensed, I reported the pervert to the principal–only to walk out minutes later–stunned by the principal's lecture which was set on rebuking my allegations and reinstating the pervert's "valuable contributions" to the school program! Incredulous and sick to my stomach, I phoned the Los Angeles Unified School District headquarters, reaching an articulate, no-nonsense black woman with an intimidating demeanor, indicating one in a high official capacity. She listened to my report while I faltered, trembling. Controlling her anger, the high official now requested the precise words used, required for official documentation. Each attempt to conjure his precise words revivified the wretched scene, increasing my fury and my inadequacy; it was no easy task to eject such filth into the ears of such a distinguished woman of rank. Fumbling and tongue-tied, I eventually gave her what she needed in spite of my disability. For the remainder of the semester, I lured my award-winning students away from that scumbag-barnyard-potty-mouth. In the safety of the greenhouse, at least the students could enjoy learning some greenhouse skills. Systems being what they are–with the pervert's aiding-and-abetting principal protecting his hide–I feared my grievance was a forlorn hope. Sensitive to a fault, I simply could not bear to follow up on the outcome, unable to bear bad news.

I took a solo journey to France for three months, hoping to wash my eyes and ears from the memory of that deplorable affair. To blend in with the scenery I traveled with a very short haircut and long skirts, celebrating my birthday in Paris. At the youth hostel I had the good fortune to meet a group of German high school girls who invited me on their bus tour to the Côte d'Azur–seeing the ancient crypts of Arles and criss-crossing the farmlands and marshes of the Camargue, famous for their spirited horses. Saying goodbye to my German hosts, I exchanged addresses with a teary-eyed Elisabeth W., who remained my loyal Wiesbaden pen pal for years running. I spent the muggy morning touring *Notre-Dame de la Garde* basilica, catching lunch at the harbor at Marseilles.

Walking the harbor of Marseille as a single female tourist, the eyes of swarthy sea dogs trolling the docks became too piercing for me. Suffering the last strange man brushing up against me unsolicited, I escaped the sailors and the assaults of diesel fumes, spotting what appeared to be a good sunning spot on the cliffs above the port. Climbing in glad expectation, the sun's thermostat was rising–all I wanted was seclusion in the sun, one safe remove from the oily fish breath of the dock.

In my leather sandals I scurried up the crags in search of a sunny nesting spot where only bird friends could find me. What looked like an oasis from afar was, on closer inspection, not more than an expanse of rocky outcroppings. I settled for less, clearing away pebbles and making a semi-soft cubby hole. Satisfied in my small success, I took off my skirt and grabbed my travel book. Stretching out my legs in my private little niche, I sighed deeply in relief. At last! Peace and quiet. Having met friends in Paris, I began reading about the area of Enghien Les Bains, in case I decided to take them up on their invitation to visit. Studying the maps, I set about to arrange a vague plan of what I most wanted to see on this new soil.

Cooking my flesh under the warm French sun, my concentration was intermittently broken, the currents feeding me signals that I was reading not more than a few lines at a time without a break.

I began to sense a peculiar, disturbing current—an *alien* current. Perturbed, I sat up to resolve the nuisance once and for all. Looking up approximately 50 feet above and behind me, I saw him.

Straddled on a rock atop the sheer cliff, I beheld the pervert—a *French Fiddler on the Roof*—violently strumming "*biddy biddy bum*" up and down the turgid shaft between his legs—the red vertex of his instrument poking and hiding in turns—the madman's eyes glazed, fixed in the crosshairs of his sights: a young American bird in a yellow bikini.

Chapter 19 Beauty Hunters

The symbol of the spirit-knowledge is a flower. The command can be communicated to the disciple from outside by a swift sending. Whereas, the spirit-knowledge blossoms from within, and cannot be evoked by any wand. Like a flower, the knowledge blooms in its destined hour. How, then, may one assist the flower? Place it in a quiet spot, give it sunlight, and forbid anyone to touch and pluck the leaves. Without the spirit-knowledge one cannot raise to its height the knowledge predestined for humanity.

El Morya

My dream of becoming a full-fledged botany nerd was near at hand. Relishing both field botany and plant taxonomy courses my first quarter at Cal Poly, I was hired the following autumn as the University's field botany plant collector, which meant I got to repeat the field trips The class was noted for its rigorous program–definitely *not* for the weak or weary. Every Friday on day-long field trips we made a thorough study of many diverse habitats throughout the tri-county area, including Santa Barbara to the south and Monterey to the north–culminating in a 3-day weekend extravaganza, to such montane uplands as Yosemite or such desert habitats as Death Valley–botanizing days and camping out nights. Two amazing professors taught the class: An ecology expert, noted for his dry humor was rounded out by the serious, nerdy type who was unexcelled in plant identification and botanical nomenclature.

As the employed botanical collector, I crowded into the bus along with 35 students for the long ride to Anza Borrego Desert in April–to study palm oases, creosote bush scrub, desert transition, chaparral, pinyon-juniper woodland and other remarkable plant communities. During the lengthy road trips, it behooved us to create our own amusement, to create our own happy-bus-ride ecosystem, as it were. The brightest students set up self-challenges to pass the hours, many of whom would become superb scholars in their varied fields of study. Not counting myself in that scholarly group, nonetheless I did become for a time thoroughly conversant with diverse taxa, intimate with the green language all around me. Impelled by a sense of sacred purpose–I was on my way to becoming a bonified botany nerd in my own right.

Sometime during the 400-mile bus ride to Anza Borrego, the ecology professor–oiling his humor wick–hit upon a great idea that did indeed take to flames of fun. Taking the microphone in hand, he put a challenge to the busload: Offering himself as judge, we were to create a nickname for his nerd colleague, the only requirement was that our terminology be akin to official botanical nomenclature. It probably was a bit daring of me to name my boss *and* major professor with such bold efficacy, but I was counting on his forgiveness. He well knew I would have sacrificed just about anything to be, just like him, perennially botanizing–nothing in the world meant more to us both. The contest was judged by those monikers evoking the loudest response. Truly looking the part of the stereotypical nerdy professor–with his coke-bottle-thick glasses and his persistent relationship with polyester trousers–I won the contest, apparently placing the nearsighted one in the proper taxonomical nomenclature: "*Myopia polyesterleggii*".

Our bus continued its brisk pace, heading to Anza-Borrego Desert, which lies between the Peninsular Ranges and the Salton Sea. An enchanting portion of the Colorado and Sonoran Deserts, *Borrego* is Spanish for the endangered bighorn sheep who make their living on the rocky slopes. Passing the miles of Creosote Bush and Mesquite, the profs pointed out the manifold coping mechanisms of the components of this ecosystem–the remarkable adaptations of desert plants whose root systems can make up to 90 percent of their total biomass. Metaphors followed suit, passing all the way to the back of the bus and back–of the similarities between desert plant survival and the human struggle for life.

Descending the mesa in our final turn, voila! Our restless eyes lit up at the spectacular presentation of Ocotillo–*Fouqueria splendens*– causing 35 students to rise from their seats in exaltation, the sparkling coral-red blooms almost blinding our eyes. Splashing vermillion on both sides of our passageway, the Ocotillo's fiery crimson transmitted baud rate flashes: Our timing was *perfecto*!

The following day we hiked down a canyon, examining soil lichens, taking photos of glamourous magenta Sand Verbena, admiring small clusters of *Brodeia*. Halting at a pool of standing water, our polyestered leader took sudden interest in the dank tinaja, which relayed to our nostrils the characteristic stench of biodegradation. As my sworn duty, I obeyed his command: I was to retrieve from the brackish slack the reed he pointed out. Partially submerged in the middle of the slough, it was perhaps a rare aquatic species– or so my boss claimed. Thinking his request a bit unusual, I paid little heed to my suspicions, duty-bound as I was. In awed silence did the students watch me, feeling sorry for the collector in the line of muddy duty, as I sloshed through the swamp water until I was, as they say–"waist high in the Hydrilla". Maintaining faithful obedience to my superior, I slogged on through the muck to pluck the "rare" reed and delivered the unknown taxa into the hands of my boss. Crowning my botanical labors with a bit of drama, he smiled mischievously, following suit with a cavalier toss: The now-suddenly-undesirable greens he sent over his shoulder, straight back into the muck–the ruse nothing more than a *Myopia polyesterleggii* payback!

Unknown to me, *instant karma* was already in the planning stages, the student body devising a prank, upping the ante to the prof's own. That night as we sat around the campfire, the polyester prankster bored us silly with his tediously long story–something to do with a mysterious, winding labyrinth inside an impenetrable fortification; something about finding the hidden key to the inner sanctorum; something about finding yet another passage and another key to enter a labyrinth. Endless and agonizingly dull–his story dragged on far longer than our patience. Some escaped the confines of the windy storyteller. They were the lucky ones: those of us waiting courteously for the punchline were duped when the punchline never came. He had lost us somewhere back there in his endless labyrinth.

Someone picked up a guitar and began strumming and singing, and the evening rolled on into the night in quiet groups. The rigorous hiking and intensity of plant adventure soon began to tell on my boss. Laying back on his backpack, he soon fell asleep, soothed by the sound of mellow guitar riffs. The next morning a photograph was passed around in hushes and starts. The image captured my nerdy boss lying next to the campfire with a blissful smile, surrounded by beer cans strewn all about him–looking very much the drunkard that he was not. For the duration of the field trip, my duties never again required entering slack ponds. Henceforth, alcohol was prohibited on all botany excursions.

The following year in the Biological Sciences department, I became the official collector for plant taxonomy labs. Loaded with special permits and a ring full of keys, I could officially pass through locked gates into remote refuges and state lands never seen by the keyless multitudes. Beauty hunting was now my *official* business. Gathering fresh taxa weekly for the labs, it was imperative that the material have diagnostic reproductive structures, essential for keying to family.

Returning from the hunt one afternoon lugging an awkward load, I made my way back slowly through the oak-woodland. Golden fields stretched out before me in a sunlight-yellow blanket, spotted here and there with accents of purple owl's clover. Heavily laden with four giant lawn bags of plant material, I fumbled constantly under the impossibly incorrigible cargo. Ecstatic with the day's hunt, I could overlook the constant stops and starts, rebalancing the unwieldy load thwarting my efforts. This time the rebounding bag caught my leg hard on the backward swing, tripping me. Kneeling in submission, I laughed at the comedic situation: my overreaching efforts were not succeeding as well as planned. Surrendering prostrate on the grassland of *Avena* and *Lollium,* I felt the ground vibrating. Looking up, I saw the source: Rumbling hooves were coming quickly my way. It was feeding time for the dozen heifers who saw the botanist with the goods in her bulging bags. The massive image of a dozen, 2,000-pound cows sent me racing the 40 yards to the gate. Without falling once, I dropped the bags at the gate–turning quickly only once, seeing the heifers closing in on me. Miraculously picking from the big ring the correct key, I made a quick getaway out that cyclone fence. Lesson learned: When conducting official botany business on state grazing lands, avoid feeding time.

A golden Toyota served me well during those tax lab years, stuffed to the roof with bags of flowering plant material. I formed the bad habit of suddenly pulling over at the sight of a flowering specimen. Angels must have been protecting me because I drove then–and still do–with my eyes half-keyed to the passing trees. In the rainy season it was a common sight to find seeds germinating in my car, the damp vinyl carpet making a surprisingly decent sprouting media. I thought it was cute, but my live-in boyfriend did not agree. Jay kept saying his *guy* stuff about resale value. What did I care about resale value? The car was there to multitask for *me*, not the other way around. Guys are like that when it comes to cars, they can't help it. Putting emphasis on cars was a waste of my time; my only concern is that my vehicle carry me–safe and sound–to my next botanical destination.

I confess. I was a bit excessive in my zeal for the green. My carloads caused protests from my colleague who had the responsibility of setting the specimens out in the labs. I felt miffed at his protests because honoring his request for less meant doing less that my best effort–always thinking of the students who were just like me, who would appreciate the extra taxa. I continued as usual, collecting with the enthusiasts in mind—about twice the amount of flora required, until the old familiar echo of state economics resounded again. Funding for my position was cut, the onus now lay within the province of the department. The department offered me a contract position in vegetation monitoring for an Environmental Impact Statement in Morro Bay. Boring. I moved over to a position with the university's Forestry Department for the next two years, absorbed in the restoration of oaks, breathing the sylvan life of trees.

Chapter 20 Commando & The Arachnid

We see much that is far from beautiful.
When working with humanity one has to wash one's hands often.

As mountain flowers find it hard to pass even one night in a swamp,
so for you it is not easy. The enemy's stroke sounds upon the strings,
but claws cannot compose a symphony. Many darts has My Shield
diverted from you....

Simply walk forward without wincing. Withholding irritation, you
create a new sheath for the spirit. Even a steed gallops better when not
frothing.

El Morya

Two spots were open with the Agriculture Commissioner for *Inspector/Biologist* but no word came for months. Assuming the worst, it was somewhat surprising when the call came for an interview. They stationed me in the Paso Robles district field office rather than at close range; commuting from Arroyo Grande took me nearly a full hour if I maintained the speed limit, which I did–in the aftermath of two expensive speeding tickets.

Placing me out in the boondocks sent a message: "This close and no closer". I had good reasons to doubt my fitness within this strange new culture–truly a *cult* mentality: I had become employed in a watered down military training bootcamp. The Commissioner was well acquainted with my work at the university, knowing me from my state and national outreach campaigns. Introducing the hardwood regeneration issues, I was responsible for building consensus; for forming a close cooperation among local civic leaders for community reforestation projects. Extensive research studies had sounded the statewide alert: Oaks were not regenerating. San Luis Obispo County, with large expanses of oak woodland, had much to lose. Officials generously stepped up to the plate. The second year of our efforts culminated in a national symposium, the department christening me with a golden plaque with engravings: "You did it, Julie Oak!" So here I was, *Miss Quercus*, in a world of restoration–moving through the turnstile into the world of pesticide enforcement; into the days of tractors, field workers and pesticides.

A second sign of trouble entered the day I met my new supervisor. A San Joaquin Valley farm girl, very thorough and outwardly civil–she was a greenhorn–having moved up the line to her first power dream-seat. Instantly she perceived me as a threat. Under the delusion that I wanted a future with the county–at her first opportunity she would attempt to thwart that development from ever becoming a reality. Her first power move came within 8 months, at my probationary review. Intoxicated by Neptunian delusions of faux power–she moved her rook to checkmate my queen. Bad move.

Paying little attention to my supervisor, both of us were too busy learning new skills. Cross-trained to cover the varied inspection programs, I was hired on specifically in the *Pesticide Use Enforcement* program, trained by a veteran of 12 years with the county, a smart guy who answered to the name "Brown Thing". Fun-loving, sincere and honest, *Brown Thing* was patient as a saint, showing me every step, answering my rapid-fire questions without tiring. Lucky for me, I had landed the world's best mentor; his ingenuity worked wonders and I caught on quickly. Both of us having a strong work ethic, we made a great team. Dubbed "the dynamic duo", our efforts surpassed the cumulative widgets of inspectors who preferred less rigorous programs such as quarantine or farmers market.

In training mode I rode shot-gun in a Dakota truck while *Brown Thing* showed me the ropes in the realms that were to be my sole responsibility. Each day a different aspect of agriculture surfaced–a new story would unfold of the lives that labored in the dusty fields. I developed a deep respect for the stalwart souls daily working the soil, raising vegetables and grains, walnuts and grapes–laboring each summer under the searing Paso Robles sun.

In professional parlance, I had "arrived" the day my widgets began catching up with *Brown Thing's* veteran stats. Taking my job seriously, I was doing my best to make the world safer for humans and the environment. The job changed me: In the world of pesticide regulation–to gain the necessary respect to do the job–I learned to exert an unnaturally conservative demeanor. The job was also teaching me valuable lessons in harmonizing heated situations, for example, when I was called out to resolve a case of sulphur dust drifting off-site, provoking two neighbors to the point of violence. A letter from one-half of the dueling farmers arrived soon after, addressed to the Ag Commissioner, commending my service rendered in mediating a resolution between the dueling brothers. The proud Commissioner drove the hour north to offer me his personal congratulations.

I garnered a second round of applause simply by providing ground safety clearance for a pilot spraying barley from his fixed-wing–a Class I organophosphate. My efforts to bar traffic from the aerial spray application landed me a letter from the thankful pilot, who wrote the Commissioner thanking him. The pilot had never before come across county staff willing to provide this level of safety. Again, the Commissioner met with me, honored and smiling.

The night before my 8-month probationary review, I dreamed a black widow spider with electric blue markings was stalking me. The next day the spider appeared in the physical, in the form of my supervisor. Sitting across from each other on a picnic table under a large valley oak, perhaps 25 meters distant from the field office–the private setting allowed the petite *Arachnid* uninterrupted space to prepare herself accordingly. Thus, she began weaving a *Kafkaesque* web of the most bizarre proportions.

"Your work in the field demonstrates to us that you are incapable of maintaining professional distance from your client-base," the *Arachnid* began pertly, avoiding eye contact. Astonished, my mouth was rent wide at her opening sting, the sharp venom numbing my wits temporarily.

"These letters from your clients are clear evidence demonstrating to us your inability to uphold a stance appropriate for enforcement," she sang primly, her left hand dancing in a circular motion on top of my review, her spider-fingers increasing in acceleration as they rotated around the form of the letters praising me.

"Excuse me!" I protested, rejecting the inanity of her verbal scum. "The Commissioner drove up personally to congratulate me on my field presence. He was honored by these letters!"

Intoning her curse in a low voice, her left hand began dancing again, circling my review in counter-clockwise rotation, the spider-fingers now accelerating their movement around the letters praising me.

"We have discussed this issue" she smiled–implicating the Commissioner, still avoiding eye contact. Deflecting, she moved operations. Her mouth curled up slightly in a sinister wickedness, her eyes now gazing beyond me as though I was not present at the table. "As well, your performance stats indicate your inability to assume the required workload," she injected, her chelicerae lusting for blood.

"We have discussed this issue and are looking into a resolution," she threatened me, with the unmistakable air of a bureaucrat. Trying hard to maintain her power, I noticed her eyeballs moving about, no longer able to avoid my eyes completely. Losing some momentum in the tremulous web of her own making, she now appeared as someone gone completely mad.

"What *are* you talking about? Obviously, you have't bothered to verify my stats, because if you had–you would have discovered that I'm working at a 70% level of an Ag III!" I challenged the *Arachnid* forcefully. Packing lies on top of lies, the creature sitting across from me began to look positively insane. Did she really think she could intimidate me with this preposterous B.S.? How someone this deceitful had made it to a supervisory level was beyond my comprehension.

It was just as my dream had foretold: A black widow assassin, working in strange, calculated rhythms, was indeed bent on assailing her probationer. Unbalanced in mind, the spider's ineptitude, her voodoo currents—just plain made me pissed off. Fortifying her death-to-the-probationer concoction by changing tactics, she kept her dark momentum alive by her constant stirring. In counter-clockwise rotation of the left-hand path—the spider stirred, lusting for my blood. Unhitched to reality, she was certain her death blow would be fatal.

Restraining myself, I listened carefully to the remainder of her *a cappella* performance, now growing into absurd fiction. Turning my mind to better use, I analyzed her seriously flawed mental condition: I knew that she had been overlooked for the position she now held; I knew that the Commissioner's first choice had turned down the offer. I knew also that the Arachnid, alone, held the current licensing. Not only was she *not* the Commissioner's choice for power queen; she had obtained the position by default.

Patiently awaiting her soliloquy to reach its faulty conclusion, I beheld her as a pathetic soul, sick from the disease of ignorance and malicious malpractice. Surveying the sad patient before me, I summed up five words to offer her.

"You are one...sick...F--K! I said calmly, looking straight into her eyes. When she didn't flinch I had to wonder if she even heard me. Noting that my supervisor was no longer fiddling with the review papers before her, I sat bemused watching the person across from me looking at nothing and no one in particular—seemingly transfixed, lost in her own web. I ventured to go a step further with the assassin, to put her out of her misery—this time in the guise of a psychiatric counselor, *"Nurse Ratched"*:

"I happen to know who was the Commissioner's first pick for your position," I began, unemotionally. "I know you were not the first pick, and now I can understand why," I finished, watching for some kind of reaction from the zombie-spider. Being a true statement, it was potent anti-venom, a poison shaft with brutal consequences.

The venomous spider changed suddenly, into a fearful child, utterly lost in the wilderness. The change came so swiftly, I could not bear to look at the mess I'd made. I left her sitting there, tears dripping down–blurring the ink on her official probationary report.

I made an appointment to see the Commissioner a.s.a.p.. Explaining my supervisor's flawed report, I showed my commander the proof: My supervisor had not bothered to look at my inspection widgets. With a quick look at the data I figured I could rest my case. Whatever thoughts may have been lurking behind the Commissioner's receding hairline, his irksome perennial smile masked them. His advice was simply that I take the high road, that I low-key the issue.

"Try to consider this for what it is: her first supervisory review," he said, showing a toothy smile. "Sometimes it's the professional thing to just agree to disagree. I would advise you to just let this one go. In the future work with her toward building good communications."

Speechless, I leaned forward, troubled by his insouciance. A few more rounds with him gained me nothing but a hollow, irrational spin. Seeing the case dismissed, I straightened my spine. Sprouting up like a beanstalk, I appealed directly to the myopic commander-in-chief:

"You're in a position to resolve this, but you will not. If you are unwilling to correct this problem–then you leave me with no other option than to go above you. Is that what you want?" I asked him, positioned in body language that comes naturally with righteous self-respect.

Strange to say, his response was nothing more than another beguiling grin. Unwilling to put his hand in the cookie jar, he preferred the issue to vanish from his desk. Apparently, falsifying a review wasn't worthy of his time. Outfitted as he was daily–in pinstripe suits– one had the impression that he would be more comfortable in the politics of Sacramento, behind closed doors. Perhaps he didn't believe I would actually go above his head. Perhaps no probationer had ever dared question his authority before.

Like a lioness, I marched downtown to a higher level in the civic hierarchy, certain that justice would prevail. With my official stats and letters of recommendation in hand, I put forth to the judges "Exhibits A and B". Ruling overwhelmingly in my favor, my supervisor was required to revisit and revise my review to reflect reality. Constrained by the imminent self-sabotage in doing such a thing, her revision showed a blatant refusal to correct her flagrant "misrepresentations". Instead, the revision seemed to come from the inchoate confusion of an embattled anarchist–a miasma of babble.

Like a lioness, I marched again to the officer judging the case, who likewise could make no sense of the drivel before her. Making her final judgment, I was to write my own review! Not a good start for a budding supervisor on her first tour on duty. Both the Commissioner and my supervisor were docked: Twin bullet-holes now marred their professional standing, their misbehavior documented on indelible microfiche–to remain in perpetuity downtown as a kind of *priors* in the halls of higher authority. It's a funny thing about politicians–the Commissioner maintained a starched smile throughout the ordeal and afterwards–acting as if nothing had ever happened.

Two years hence, my request to fill a vacancy in the central office finally materialized. My new cubicle was in full view of the real-time, nuts-and-bolts of the central hub, where I could view the starched and perennially smiling commander more closely. I noted that his every dictate was funneled through a fuzzy network of agents, after long talks behind closed doors. He was rarely seen, except at his boring "ice cream socials" which he seemed to rather enjoy.

I had a keen respect for my new supervisor, whose knowledge of the law was impeccable. Her indefatigable work ethic seemed a model for the cause. Impassive and unyielding when acting as an expert judge in pesticide enforcement hearings, her presence in the county influenced local agriculture most decidedly. Tough as dragon teeth in the field she was known as the "Queen of Mean", an unfair moniker for one who dedicated her whole life to a worthy cause. I was an expert witness at a hearing when the Queen spewed her famous blowtorch–singeing a perpetrator for his egregious pesticide malpractice, slapping the wretch with huge fines. Immediately jerked from his job, word came through the mill that the violator took off to Thailand; he was heard to say that pesticide regulation over there was lax.

Late one afternoon, the inspectors were called, en masse, to the central office for a meeting. Our commander-in-chief wanted our collective thoughts on his proposal to solve a local environmental problem and sent his agent to approach us on the issue: Pine pitch canker, a *Fusarium* fungus. The disease had literally killed off most of the native pines (and would eventually make a transgeneric jump to Douglas fir). Flyers from CDF were circulated, advising isolation, hermetic sealing and containment of diseased trees. There was no question–the fungus posed a very serious situation.

The puncture vine was also raised, a serious local problem; a noxious weed spreading on road shoulders throughout the county. This was the second point of discussion. The idea being floated to us for consideration was in the nature of a financial gain, a joint effort together with CalTrans: CalTrans would chip the pine pitch cankered trees into a mulch. That mulch would then be used to cover the puncture vine, ostensibly inhibiting growth of the puncture vine. The Ag Depatment's road crew would function as the mulcher, depositing the fungus-ridden tree mulch throughout the county roadsides!

As the commander's messenger-agent voiced the preposterous idea, I panicked, in a heart-brain triple synapse–looking around the room for colleagues who perceived the proposition as ill-advised as I did. I found only one, a silent dissenter. Sapped from the brain drain of the heavy workload, the group was unable to sense the lunacy of the proposal and too tired to give a damn. Having been repudiated for my independent thoughts at these meetings, I was reluctant to be the first to speak. I sat there thinking to myself that the head bimbos in this joint are ready to spread disease throughout the county, and maybe the state, so long as it brings financial gain! I looked around the room again, searching each of the 15 faces around the table. Was anyone else awake? No one came forward. I had to voice my concern. I did not hold back my angst, but tried to soften my personal disapproval with the rank and file. I let semi-loose on the pernicious proposal which posed an insurmountably disastrous injurious potential. Not only would it spread contamination and upset the natural ecology—but would most likely land the county in a string of lawsuits.

The next morning I was not surprised when I was called in for insubordination, the commander-in-chief sending his agent to do his bidding for him. Entering the agent's office, I found him sitting stiffly upright, looking ominously tall behind his big desk. I was not offered a seat.

"I hear you have a problem with our program," he stated flatly, his squinting icy blue eyes steaming with latent heat. He intended to intimidate me.

"You bet I do!" I blasted back righteously, not in the least concerned for my fate. "Why do we distribute CDF flyers advising the public on the dangers of the disease and then go against our own rules? I don't understand the logic here, this is a very scary proposition."

His rebuttal had something to do with a professor from the University—a Ph.D "expert" whose research data showed the potential fungal contamination to be nil. Such was the entire basis of the counter-argument! Ha! I knew a little something from four years of college biology. Idiotic ideas can and do originate from credentialed idiots.

I was the antonymic opposite of a lemming: I followed no idea simply because a credentialed "expert" espouses it to be so. I found the whole business incredulous—dangerous, and I let it be known, regardless of the repercussions. Our meeting did not last long. Neither did the dicey proposal; it was aborted and never a word spoken again. They didn't know what to do with me. The commander found me "overwhelming." So be it. He certainly couldn't complain about my work ethic. I stayed on because I liked working with farmers and ranchers and providing safety for field workers who didn't know the hazards of the pesticides they handled. I loved being outdoors, riding in my Dakota to unknown, remote wildernesses. I challenged myself to stay put for five long years.

Exactly three weeks before that five-year term came to a close, a string of strange incidents emerged their ugly little heads. Sniffing the miasma of subterfuge, I decided to ignore it, carrying on as usual, exited at the upcoming separation which promised to trade my "pesticide cop" badge for more creative work. Behind the scenes my Commando-in-chief was deep into intrigue: In his haste, he had plans to take a parting shot at me, hoping to "brand" me, apparently because I had "branded" him and tarnished his county record–scoring him a demerit due to his foolish behavior in his handling of my probationary review. My guess is that Commando hoped to cast aspersions on my reputation, thereby nullifying somewhat my claims against him. What a farce! The Commando failed miserably. Again. *Instant karma* would take him even further downstream, treading and finally drowning in the waters of despair: In the end he discovered that he was only a very small fish in a very big pond–not the Alpha shark in pinstripes he fantasized.

Setting me up for a fall using two of his agents to frame me in a safety issue, the Commando proved inept as an undercover operative. The problem came to an abrupt end, due to the fact that he cast a God-fearing, orthodox Christian in the role of the hangman–the one who's *lie* was required in order to put me in violation. When it came time for showdown, the God-fearing churchman simply could not find it in his heart to tell a lie. At the precise moment–a moment pregnant with potential injury–the churchman paused, and demurred. It was a curious thing to watch him get one big dose of the holy spirit which–quite suddenly–put me in full charge of the questioning from then on–once again having to write my own review!–proving myself absolved of any wrongdoing. The pertinent "violation" at issue with my accusers was whether I *was* or *was not* wearing the required safety boots when walking through a pesticide-laden field during inspection. The ridiculous fiasco I took to the upper hierarchy, who by now knew me on a first-name basis. The poor churchman! He was unceremoniously dumped, pushed out of his job soon after the incident–moving his Christian family many miles away. Not cut out for the big league intrigues, the nest of the pin-striped Commando proved too much for the churchman's clean spirit.

Some years later, the Commando would find himself in deep *doodoo*–again, triggering a homemade "detonation device" which ended in self-destruction. The guy had a penchant for creating monsters of his own undoing. This time he hyped up a fantasy crime–*ala* Hollywood–attempting to shake down a grower. It was a well known fact that the Commando had built a strong disliking to this grower–a personal vendetta? Acting way outside county protocol, the Commando called the FBI in on the investigation: Suited up with guns, the Feds screeched onto the farm and shut down the operation, taping the "crime scene" in yellow and holding everyone for questioning. Bad move: This marked the beginning of the end for the Commando. Sentenced by a vote of "No Confidence," Commando proved just too big a liability for the county. Removing him out of his commanding position and shuffling him around for a bit, Commando suffered a humiliating expulsion–terminated by the State and hung out to dry like French laundry.

Power is a dangerous thing in the hands of those hungry for it, that is to say: those lacking *inner* power, who grab on to an outer substitute. If one is lacking *inner* power, that one lacks an inner guidance system. Power is not a toy for personal gain, it is a responsibility, to be used only for the greater good.

Chapter 21   King Arthur

I know a bank where the wild thyme blows,
Where oxlips and the nodding violet grows,
Quite over-canopied with luscious woodbine,
With sweet musk-roses and with eglantine.

William Shakespeare. A Midsummer Night's Dream (Act ii. Scene.1)

The Mother of the World appears as a symbol of the feminine Origin in the new epoch, and the masculine Origin voluntarily returns the treasure of the World to the feminine Origin.

Amazons were the embodiment of the strength of the feminine Principle, and now it is necessary to show the aspect of spiritual perfection of woman.

The lofty mission of women must be performed by the woman. And in the Temple of the Mother of the World should abide the woman. The manifestation of the Mother of the World will create the unity of women. The task now is to create a spiritually sovereign position for the woman. And the transmission to woman of direct communication with the Highest Forces is necessary as a psychological impetus. Of course, through the new religion will come the necessary respect.

El Morya

It was June. I was at peace. I sat often in meditation here on the rise–400 feet above sea level. Overlooking the sleepy artist hamlet of Halcyon to the west, Arroyo Grande to the north–to the east lay acres of vineyards tucked between miles of oak-woodlands. Looking straight down from my meditation mountain lay eyefuls of beautiful black soil, patterned with crucifers and lettuce in annual rotation. Row upon perfect row, greens were cultivated in the expert hands of Isei Japanese farmers and their Nisei sons. Just beyond the broccoli and Bok Choy patchwork stretched a peridot green ocean, lapping the sands of the Pismo-Oceano Dune complex.

Red shouldered and Red tailed hawks called this bluff their home, the Red shouldered's piercing "kee-aah" defending their fair share from his larger Buteo brother. From above the towering windbreak of *Eucalyptus globulus* came flying the aerial acrobats–the Buteos harvesting the bumper crop of rodents, hiding in my landlord's irrigated *Vinca major* which commanded a thick border on both sides of a driveway running 1/3 mile up to the two homesites. The entire 32 acres was a rodentian retreat, keeping my cat entertained, his daily portion proffered by myriad pocket gophers.

Our isolated habitation was also the home address of resident Anna's hummingbirds, the Rufous-sided occasionally making a showing. "King" Arthur, as we sometimes called my landlord, was made famous through a news article captioned: "The Hummingbird Man". The local television station followed up, filming the metallic ruby-and-green hummers swarming around Arthur's oversized feeder, their co-star and benefactor standing proud as a father-mother caretaker alongside his diminutive minions, frenzied in their flight to the sugar water. Eyes twinkling for the camera, the devoted caretaker chronicled the 20-year man-and-birds love affair, his 200-pound frame making a stark contrast to the Lilliputian loves of his life.

A wonderfully silly septuagenarian, Arthur was a gentle soul and quite distinct from his lineage of upper class, east-coast military gentry. His niece and her husband lived down the road apiece, making for a small band of friends on King Arthur's acres. Arthur admired my philosophy and lifestyle, occasionally eliciting my views on his life work: The non-proliferation of nuclear weapons. An admirable work, I listened to his ideas while I dug soil, preparing my garden–working mulch and peat moss into the sandy substrate. At these times Arthur would remind me to be on the lookout for Indian middens: mortars and pestles, clam and shellfish–remains of the indigenous tribe who once sheltered on the site. The northern *Obispeño Chumash* Indians had been prevalent in the area as far back as possibly 5,000 years ago. Arthur explained the demise of the Chumash after their contact with the Spaniards, beginning with the 1542 Spanish exploration and again in 1769-1770 with the Portolá expedition. It was highly possible, Arthur believed, that they moved right through the ground on which we were standing. His description of the Mission San Luis Obispo de Tolosa held my interest. Founded in 1772 as the first Spanish establishment in Chumash territory, within 30 years the mission housed most of the Obispeño Chumash. "Within only 30 years of the Spanish missionization," Arthur said, his sad eyes gazing out to the ocean mists, "the missionaries had introduced disease into the indigenous population, wiping out the Chumash along with their culture."

Winters on the bluff were brutal–there was nothing to break the onshore winds. My house came with a sorry excuse for a propane heater–a zero sum gain option. Set at an angle 90 degrees from a drafty, wooden door, the puny thing made a big fussy noise, barely warming the entryway. Unweatherized, the 1,200 square-foot house was built of cold slump stone that sent a chill through the porous masonry. The entire western side of my winter igloo was an expanse of single-paned, sliding glass windows, nor had the roof been properly insulated. Beautiful, but ridiculously inefficient, I survived the winters without artificial heat in the following manner: At dusk I went jogging on the steep surrounding hillocks, continuing my pace until the sweat was pouring out. Back inside the igloo, I followed up as needed–becoming a human furnace through energetic dancing. Improvising from my childhood dance lessons, I worked through a series of ballet exercises from all the positions I could remember–probably creating some originals in the process. In the privacy of my home, I practiced *relevés, pliés*

and *bourrées*. Those cold winters helped me improve my *pirouettes*: Coming from a tight third position, I *spotted* on my Grandmother's Egyptian mosaic which hung prominently on the wall. After ballet warm ups, I danced an exhilarating freestyle, alternating from the high-energy sounds of Afro-Celtic to the throaty panpipes of South America.

I was first introduced to the exotic sounds of world music at the KCBX Live Oak Music Festival in the hills behind Santa Barbara, looking forward each year to new surprises. Duane had a penchant for booking the best for the venue, movers and shakers from Peru to Zimbabwe. This Santa Barbara gig gave rise to my own hilltop gatherings, the *Fairie Fests*, beginning with the original six of us '*fairies*' who worked together as volunteers backstage at the festival. The six of us provided ambiance, transportation and security for the performers–ensuring ultra comfort for such icons as David Crosby, Jackson Browne, Bonnie Raitt, The Eagles, Sam Bush, Greg Brown and Peter Rowan–to name just a few. After our third year volunteering together, the six of us had become like family, finding it heartbreaking to part ways when the mournful Monday brought the festival to an end. I posed a solution: Hummingbird Hill! The following weekend we met up at my eyrie for a gala and sleepover event–sans children, sans husbands–female friends free to just *be*.

By the fifth year, my parties had become legendary. The *Fairie Fests* at Hummingbird Hill ran the gamut of theme costumes, clothing and jewelry exchanges, artisan demonstrations and sales, plant exchanges, and scrumptious pot-luck delectables. Crowding into my big wooden hot tub, personal stories–and intimate confessions–became a ritual. Dancing well into the night, we finally dropped from exhaustion. Being a teetotaler myself, I discouraged hazy mindlessness, finding it necessary only one time to administer restraint to the fairies. That was *not* what the event was all about. What it *was* ultimately all about–the girls, level-headed, would collectively decide each year. These mini-fest gatherings were about creative life: About the uninhibited freedom of exchanging creative ideas with noble, free-thinking friends. About intellectual discussions with creative, brilliant minds. About the epicurean enjoyment of healthy food and dance. The gatherings were soul meetings, meetings of the mind in a beautiful, natural haven. Hummingbird Hill was the place to form new and lasting friendships.

By the ninth year, my female fests had morphed into a creation of its own. From its humble beginnings of 6 world music enthusiasts–to the now upwards of 40 of the finest crop of smart, creative women I could find–the *fairie* women were ripening, coming into their own authentic fructification. Artists and musicians, lawyers and linguists, biologists and chemists, computer scientists and businesswomen–the ever-growing party list counted a brainy-to-zany ratio of perhaps 80/20. My last hill gathering was special: I decked the halls with fresh flowers galore, draping colored silk fabrics throughout the many garden niches. Sparkling white mini-lights hung throughout the trees and grounds to welcome 38 women, dressed in theme costume. This would be the year my friends gathered at the *Honeysuckle Garden* stage for an evening production of Shakespeare's *Midsummer Night's Dream*. Six-foot-tall Nell played *Hippolyta*, legendary Queen of the Amazons. Karen played the enchanting and mischievous *Puck*, who delights in playing pranks on mortals. Jo played the *Lion*, worried that his roaring might frighten the ladies in the audience. Gerry danced to flute music as *Philostrate*, carrying signage separating our scenes and Mary played the *Wall* dividing the two lovers 'who did talk through the chink of a wall'. Peggy played *Pyramus* to my *Thisbe*:

> *O grim-look'd night! O night with hue so black!*
> *O night, which ever art when day is not!*
> *O night, O night! alack, alack, alack,*
> *I fear my Thisby's promise is forgot!*

Cropping the original script at our leisure, Nell's colleague, a university literature professor, acted as our coach. How could we go wrong? One fairie attendee, dressed as Hymen, the God of marriage, remarked wittily: "It was the greatest Shakespeare ever seen on this hill!" When my boyfriend–a superb cook–returned the next morning, he fed the remaining faeries his catch of local fish. Obeying the Shakespearean edict on the invitation: 'Kinder, men and other pets are elegant, but verboten, ixnée'–Eric had camped out with a buddy after a day of fishing.

Through the years, I found that grouping female personalities for such an event was an art. Like a chemist concocting a soup–choosing additional ingredients to join the main core–one adds just enough spice to enhance. Too much spice can spoil the soup. I took chances spicing sometimes. Some spices were not added again, some spices were so appreciated, they were encouraged to bring a "friend-spice" the following year. There were times when heartfelt responses flooded the morning after a party. First-timers sometimes felt something had changed in them, felt healed by all the wonderful women. Female bonding reached new heights on the hill. One letter still brings tears to my eyes: Coming from my Chinese friend who drove from Los Angeles to be with us, she shared her heart:

Dear Julie,

This made my day by knowing you enjoyed the gift. The 4 rolls of film just went in to be developed today.

Sometime I have lots of uncertainty about life. Specially when I am up around your area, I felt calm and happy with serenity. But, once back in Los Angeles, I felt I am always busy and anxious, and afraid of something. From the party and conversation, I learned that it must come from inside, like what you have.

I am so proud that I had the experience on participating your festival.

Yi

Chapter 22   Guinness

Test them to find out where they are sufficient and where they are lacking.

Sun Tzu. The Art of War

After Eric left the hill, my Manx cat, "Guinness", became the alpha male and a champion gopher-getter. Never a day went by without that telltale gnashing sound. And never a day went by without Guinness leaving me the remains to clean up—head, intestines and liver, I believe it was. Preferring to dine indoors, his piles of gopher entrails required that I stock a ready supply of 409 carpet cleaner. Blessed be that cat's name! His only demerit was his refusal to take medication for the endless series of tape worms, resident on gophers. Trying to push pills down his throat disturbed us both.

One afternoon, after several hours in squat position, performing manual pest control lest the battalion *de escargot* should overtake my unarmed flowering civilians—I stretched out my aching knee joints to admire the return on my investment. My garden scintillated with purple, lilac and white ornamental kale. Vigorously washing my snail-snotted hands, I peered at the frothing heap filling half the volume of a 5-gallon bucket. Not bad, not bad for a couple hours' work, I thought, sending up a prayer for the French immigrants before delivering them to my neighbor's ducks for dinner.

Hearing a skirmish, I located my escargot in the shade before making my way towards the commotion, betting fairly that my cat was busy catching another gopher. Coming into view was indeed this feline truth: Guinness was in a stand-off—facing the largest gopher I had ever seen. Standing erect on hind legs in a quasi toe-shoe arabesque, this was no ordinary gopher. This tribal elder, a grisly survivor, stood more than 2 feet high, towering above my poor little Guinness—and he meant business, hissing and thrusting in threatening spurts. I feared he might be a ferocious gang leader who had lived to tell his grandchildren his stories as a victorious cat conqueror. This guy was a veteran and an ugly one, too–with long, filthy greenish teeth. Holding his long body erect, the rodent remained steady, in fighter position–ominous, his eyes pinned on Guinness. Yes, it was his eyes that frightened me. O, my heart.

Guinness studied the rodent carefully. Not exactly haughty, he still worked the gopher as if he had a long-range plan. Circling slowly around the buck-tooth gopher, Guinness put in a fast right and then jabbed a quick left–working the gopher, moving him around in a circle, surveying his prey. From a calculated distance–each thrust was aimed expertly to hit the mark. Guinness thrusted and retreated, repeating his feline art for what seemed an eternity. Unnerved, I could not bear the frightening scene any longer. Retreating into the house, I did not want to be the cause for Guinness to lose concentration, thinking *veterinarian*. Watching from the window I realized I was witnessing a remarkable demonstration of raw martial arts in its feral aspect. I could not help but admire Guinness, whose prowess could not have been improved upon had he studied from Sun Tzu's *The Art of War*:

'*Test them to find out where they are sufficient and where they are lacking*

When it is disadvantageous for either side to go forth, it is called standoff terrain.

On standoff terrain, even though the opponent offers you an advantage, you do not go for it–you withdraw, inducing the enemy half out, and then you attack, to your advantage...

Sizing up opponents to determine victory, assessing dangers and distances, is the proper course of action for military leaders. Those who do battle knowing these will win, those who do battle without knowing these will lose.'

Chapter 23 California Winegrapes

Healer, tell the ailing ones that the use of wine diminishes by half their chances, that the use of narcotics takes away three quarters of their vitality. Certainly in My pharmacy there is no place for narcotics. Before using My medicines one must spend three years amidst prana.

A being who possesses full vitality is in no need of inoculations; he has the so-called solar immunity.

El Morya

Every 40-something lawyer, accountant or executive with disposable income wanted a shot at making their own wine in the mid-90s. That required planting a vineyard. A vineyard requires baby grapevines. Paso Robles and Santa Barbara were two hotspots getting most of the attention.

I got a call from an Arroyo Grande wholesale nursery, a large operation with sprawling acreages of greenhouses and more money than God. The president and I had been friends for years, both of us having similar philosophies and pioneering spirits. He asked me to set up a greenhouse production venture in *winegrape benchgrafts*. The president's reputation for genius had gained him status as consultant to the United Nations–so brains and money we had. It was the technology information–the industry secrets– we lacked. Never mind that we had no idea how to start; that's what pioneers do. From day one I knew I was in for a wild ride. What I didn't know was how difficult it would be to obtain inside information. Tight-lipped competitors, 13 of them, wished we would just go away–they certainly weren't about to help us in our chancy venture. Without the inside trade secrets, it would be folly to proceed: Benchgrafting grapevines is an art filled with untold challenges. To begin with I needed to find out things like: Which rootstocks graft best with which clones and which combinations fail; which rootstocks work in which soil types; how long to heal the graft and at what temperatures; who had certified wood and who had "dirty" wood; when to look for latent virus on potential sources...the list was endless.

The most crucial question was whether we could gear up in time to see a ROI. There was only a 2- to 3-year frenzied window of opportunity; after that, a glut was expected, potentially grinding the whole business to a halt. Once we gained some traction, the viability check seemed to be a reasonable bet. Long supplying the market with benchgrafts, 13 established nurseries had cemented firm relationships with growers. The biggest players were vying for a chunk of the local action and not one of them would sell me even a stick of grapestock–and without sticks we could not enter the ring. Thanks to my years with the county, I checked in with my grower contacts, eventually developing sources for both scion and rootstock.

Trade secrets were assiduously kept. To say it was difficult to eke out industry secrets is to utter a gross understatement. It helped somewhat by attending U.C. Davis viticulture short courses and dozens of workshops throughout the Tri-County viticulture appellations. Persistence paid the dividends as vital information came forth. As privileged intelligence began to trickle in, I learned the host of issues facing all nurseries: A debilitating 50% mortality in the greenhouse had come to be expected in many cases, causing more than a little chaos among the industry. The emotional cost to shorted growers was whispered about in huddled circles, when yet another grower was forced to wait an additional season for the contracted allotment. Now on the inside, I heard the horror stories of sizable nursery losses, of expectant vintners making house calls to check on their baby vines.

UC Davis' certification program performed the "litmus" test for grapestock disease, but the art of benchgrafting was still ascending a steep learning curve. Imported varieties were another issue– with some sticks coming through quarantine, while others were smuggled in. The year we entered the game, the average SOP for benchgrafting–to compensate random losses–was a 20%-50% industry-wide overgraft, depending on various factors. Strange to say, our nursery experienced very little loss. I attributed this to the fact we had all women doing the work. There being 32 sequential steps to benchgrafting grapevines, the entire process requires the finest care and delicate handling. We guaranteed our product; these contracts were high dollar investments for both the greenhouse operation as well as the vineyard owners.

Our first year, the big boys weren't too concerned because they received the prize orders, while I secured the smaller contracts. We did a smart thing: we grew spec plants to give out as sample product for trial planting. By our second year, we were noticed. Securing a booth at the ASEV in Sacramento, the big boys sent their scouts to visit our booth, to have a look at our product. Taking a long hard look at the enlarged root capacity of our benchgrafts, they could witness up close the truth which we claimed in our marketing brochure:

"Our 8" depth growing tube, designed in concert with European engineering, provides the sturdiest and most extensive root system on the benchgraft market today…"

Orders started coming in. I had to move fast, sourcing rootstock from 7 different counties. Our "Omega" grafts suffering only insignificant losses, we more often came out with a clean sweep of 100% vibrant green baby soldiers. I loved to watch the faces of growers–bug-eyed in wonder–amazed at seeing row after greenhouse row full of flawless viable product.

The most daunting task of all was to secure absolutely clean wood, free from disease. Many varieties are asymptomatic, showing no obvious signs of virus at certain times of the year. The list of insects and pathogens was endless: Root phylloxera, Pierce's Disease, Eutypa, Black Goo, Crown Gall, Leaf Roll, Fan Leaf Virus, Rupestris Stem Pitting, Dagger nematode... it never ended.

Never working less than a 10-hour day–my hours were split between my home office, meeting growers in the vineyards, and coordinating operations in the greenhouse which, fortunately was only a 10-minute drive from Hummingbird Hill. In my white 4x4, I gathered grapewood from vineyards for the president's perennial experiments. Some vineyards had no location on any county map. Venturing onto freshly irrigated clay roads I expected to get stuck at times. One morning driving through one of our source vineyards in Shandon, I got myself stuck in the mud. Digging myself in deeper, the rabbits and chipmunks were the only ones witnessing my ineptitude–the only ones around at 5am. Too proud to call the vineyard manager for help, I finally managed to free myself by shoving wooden planks behind my tires. Driving up to the office with my budsticks, the manager laughed it off sweetly. He was right: My white truck did look as though it had been sprinkled in a chocolate factory.

Wine enthusiasts are a social bunch. To get vineyard contracts, I had to show up at social events. My competitors always did. Marketing extravaganzas, wine tastings, field short courses–there was always some winegrape event to attend. Marketing a new product and facing stiff competition, there was a period of adjustment–how I was going to deal with the endless social cycles of the industry. Since I did not drink alcohol, I was at a potential loss trying to do business with a potential client opening his third bottle of Shiraz. I dared not offend with a refusal. Typically, I would request white wine, pour it down the sink and fill it back up with water. They were usually too sauced; no one ever knew the difference.

The truth was that I did *not* enjoy the social side of the drinking crowds. Always the botany nerd, I preferred the research and development side and eagerly sought out these opportunities. I knew my limits: When I reached my social tolerance threshold, I needed to escape, preferring to avoid the presence of all human beings for at least 24 hours, if possible.

Chapter 24   Jehovah's Witnesses

It is difficult for a dove to fly in the fog. I lead you by the speediest path and at the moment of obscuration I am ready to send a messenger. But open the doors to him; it is difficult to stand knocking in the rain.

When you feel the manifestation of an achievement, then remember that a wondrous thread is incandescing. My Soul rejoices to realize that none will stop you. I am sending you joy; show attention. Manifest calmness; the convulsion will end.

El Morya

On my way out to Adelaida to check on a potential client, I stopped in Paso Robles to catch a session on organic winegrape growing. Arriving early, I spotted my good friend, an organic grower from Templeton. Pouring me a cup of coffee, he motioned me over to the door where we could speak privately. Savoring the news of a nice contract I had just landed, my friend knew the Santa Barbara grower well. Consulting me on sourcing Mourvedre and Counoise budsticks, my friend's attention was drawn to a tall, graceful, 40-ish man entering the meeting room.

"Who is this?" the handsome stranger inquired, walking up to us. Introductions made, my friend backed up a step, while the tall stranger took my hand in a welcome gesture. Searching my eyes, he seemed to place some past connection with me; perhaps I reminded him of someone. Maintaining a firm grasp of my hand, he continued to look deeply into my eyes but remained mute. After some time, the intensity of his gaze began to excavate my social shyness too deeply. I cut his questioning eyes off. "No, I don't believe we have met before," bringing him back to the present.

At that first eyeful—the moment of visual contact—a mysterious bond was forged between us. With each future meeting our bond strengthened, amplified in a remarkable intensity. There was no escaping the power of the electro-magnetic current of attraction. But the attraction remained at arms-distance; a secret between just the two of us. He was married. Devoted to his wife and children, I likewise had high morals, and kept to the straight path. No physical touch, no direct affection; only the eyes could speak. It must be kept a secret, not a word could be exchanged between us. This unspoken pact made the attraction all the more intense, painful. Words cannot adequately describe the compounding effects of silence + romance + intensity + mystique + passion + desire + pain. Forbidden. Lonely erotica.

Then I received a sign. The signs I trust come to me when deep in Kriya Yoga meditation. In this particular sitting, I was questing for the higher meaning of the silent romance, needing a better understanding of the mystifying relationship. Did it serve a purpose? Why did I stay in a place so excruciatingly intense and painful, not to mention alone? In a deep, contemplative state, I began to hear, and then feel the earth trembling and rumbling below me. Following the commotion, I beheld a herd of Elephants rushing into view in my *third eye*. Elephants are symbolic of a universal force so incomprehensibly powerful–there is no force more powerful, no equable opposing force. Nothing whatsoever could stop the momentum of the rushing herd. Willing myself–by pranic breathing–to maintain a meditative poise of perfect silence, I allowed the dramatic stimulus entering me to pass quickly. As the thought-form vanished, I entered into a complete stillness– long enough for my body's sensoria to fully detach from the *idea* that had just minutes ago stormed my citadel. In that pure silence "which passeth all understanding," the vision's message became undeniably clear. Seeming to come from nowhere and everywhere simultaneously, I heard the sending, a word clearly pronounced: "inexorable," informing me that a karmic bond from the past was at issue. Unstoppable as nature herself, that karmic bond had surfaced, to be replayed on the stage of the present lifetime.

This marked the beginning of a whole new paradigm. From this point on in this autobiography, I would not expect the casual reader to understand the experiences–unusual as they appear to the uninitiated. But that matters little to me. Someday everyone will be spiritual scientists, developing spiritual senses, glimpsing the reality of the higher, invisible octaves. At some time in the future, everyone will feel and touch a different reality. Practicing the silence of meditation develops the clear window of consciousness, through which emerges this reality, this raw Self-truth. It is a question of one's bearing: Is the soul strong enough to receive the truth? When the student is ready the truth will come.

Inexpressible desires. It has its own language. The pressure needs to find release. Bridging the gap of silence, my secret admirer used ingenious methods to hear my voice. Since I dealt daily with an "invisible" public, answering inquiries on our nursery product, my fantasy lover saw his opportunity. His associate called me one afternoon while my lover listened from another phone. The associate wanted me to pick up that the call was on behalf of my lover. He was a reasonable sort, so I went along with it. I can't recall precisely the context, but when he used the word "Pacekeeper", I got pissed. My secret lover and I were both Alphas, but it was becoming evident he wanted to call all the shots. "Pacekeeper" meant he was in control of the *Pace*, deciding when I get my next love lollipop. I was in too deep of pain to ignore this thoughtless remark. How dare he! I took a deep breath and, rather haughtily, counter-attacked: "*Pace*-keeper....hmmm...Is that anything like Pace-*MAKER*?!

Lying on the couch one Sunday morning in my forest green velvet robe, I put down my coffee cup in order to drift off into the land of eroticism. I was several hundred pages into that inspired book by Marion Zimmer Bradley, *Mists of Avalon,* and could not put the book down. When I finally did, I put my hands on my southern parts, bringing myself to several orgasms. Obsessing orgiastically on my handsome stranger, inspired by Bradley's recent pages, I could not keep my hands off myself–imagining us in various positions, together on horseback being one of my finest erotic moments. I could not seem to get enough, there was no end in sight to my fantasies. His intelligent eyes were enough to drive me mad. His subtly commanding body language made me quiver. A big player in the industry, he was a heavyweight challenge. I wanted him to devour my body.

Lost in the depths of Eros, with my hand setting my body to quivering again–I was interrupted by a strong hand rapping hard on the front door. Not bothering to wash my hands, I wiped the moist threads of silken musk onto my white panties and sauntered to the door in a half-conscious state, dreaming of lust. Curling a breezy, faraway smile I opened the door without thinking twice. I figured, from the masculine strength–the familiar knock must be my contractor neighbor, Gregg–a good friend who visits from time to time. Much to my surprise, there stood two men, one black, one white–dressed in Sunday suits–ostensibly witnesses making a house call on behalf of Jehovah. Catching me totally unaware, my face muscles automatically tightened in girlish embarrassment. Hastening to belt my robe more snugly, I turned away from my visitors to rearrange my mental bearing. Thinking of the men of religion and the uncanny juxtaposition of them catching me in such a blithering state of ecstasy, I tried several times to assuage my guilt. Recovering my wits, I melted into hospitality mode on behalf of the two witnesses.

It occurred to me briefly that it was highly unusual to receive such visitors on Hummingbird Hill, which required just under two miles on a gravel road. I looked around for their car and found none. Before I could form the question, the taller of the two gentlemen began his line of questioning: What did I believe in? Did I pray? Barely letting me finish, he fired another question, leaving me little time to think on any track other than his. Before I realized what was taking place, I had innocently followed the man's track–freely speaking my mind. Further and further was I being led onto the stage, performing for their edification an endearing commentary on the great teacher, Paramahansa Yogananda. I spoke of how the Hindus practice the only true religion–no religion at all! As the taller one continued feeding me questions, drawing me out, I spoke of how meditation alone brings us the divine laws of the Universe. One of his injunctions compelled me to alert him that dogmas keep souls living inside of a box, shielding them from the truth.

A shift in the air currents took hold. It was then that I understood what was happening: the tall man had been working on my energy field, my aura. I could feel his magnetism striking me, compelling me to empty my soul completely. He had an enormous power over me, pulsing strong currents of energy onto my aura–activating my naturally effusive nature. He was purposely compelling me to either examine myself deeply, or perhaps he might have been testing my moxie, to find out what I was really made of. Either way, I noticed his eyes: They were all wrong. Strange to say, his eyes were definitely not fully joined into the sockets completely, especially his right eye. He was watching me very closely. I looked away, somewhat befuddled, yet curious–unable to make sense of the bizarre presentation of the loose eyeballs.

Somewhat nervous, I turned away from the tall intense man, and for the first time looked at the face of his solemn associate. He had not spoken one word. Never did. This one emanated peace, perfect peace, I thought, smiling at his gentle eyes–eyes which seemed to melt together with mine, in a sense of knowingness. There was something familiar about the man of peace, something about his soul. As our eyes joined, I began moving forward involuntarily towards the gentle one–drawn into the deep pool of his eyes, the mirror of the soul. Subsumed into the vortex of his love, I was experiencing the same sensation as when flying into the matrix of my music book. Moving into the soul of his eyes, I almost lost my balance, causing me to turn away, later regretting my cowardice, wondering what I missed had I stayed my ground.

What is happening here? Who *are* these people? My landlord had been playing with his llama in the corral. Anyone coming to my house would have had to pass right by him for a full 1/3 mile. According to Arthur–a man with all his faculties in tact–absolutely no car came up the driveway. It would be some time before I would recognize their pictures and discover their true identity. These two would become my spiritual preceptors. Known as the *Mahatmas of the Himavat*, both had ascended from earth more than 100 years ago. They were members of the spiritual hierarchy, a Brotherhood of beings who remain in the etheric octaves above Earth, postponing their higher evolution–in order to assist mankind.

Chapter 25   White Bird

White bird,
In a golden cage, alone.
White bird must fly or she will die.
White bird must fly or she will die.
White bird must fly or she will die.

It's a beautiful day

Never will I choose a calm surface of water;
rather will I accept all thunderings,
and My Scrolls, as lightnings, will transform the Dome of the Universe.
I will send a dove as messenger but I will descend as the Eagle!
Thus, let each of My warriors prepare his armor!

El Morya

In my office on my hill, I contacted the single nurseryman who would sell me budsticks. Sourcing Dijon clones on the phone, I sat listening to my long-winded friend discuss the particulars of his Burgundian budwood. I needed Pinot Noir clones 113, 114, 115, 667, and 777. Working out specific details of the contract, he faxed me a copy to check over. With the scion business completed, we moved the discussion to trends changing the industry and sources to stay clear from–truly a kind fellow, willing to help me in any way he could. I felt fortunate to find such inside help and expressed my appreciation to him.

Saying my thanks to my gracious friend, my eyes were drawn by a flash of white moving in the garden, near the *Buddleya* shrub about 15 feet from me. Something large and white was moving around in back of the Butterfly Bush. Coming into clear view, that *something* was a very large bird–pure white. The white bird began scratching like a chicken as if looking for worms and soil grubs. While the nurseryman on the line droned on, I watched in amazement as the bird turned to face me. Looking straight at me, his big white body now looked more like a swan. Yet, when he turned, his profile looked just like dove! It was becoming complicated–I couldn't figure it out. In between occasional remarks to the nurseryman, my mind was racing through all the birds I had studied in ornithology class. Mentally running through my bird list, no species lingered as a potential hit; every possibility quickly vanished. It had to be an exotic bird from some other country, I thought. But what was it doing here in my garden? Was it lost? No, the bird was obviously domesticated, showing a definite personality, even a sense of humor. It was obvious this bird was quite comfortable around humans. I watched in wonderment as the white chicken-swan-dove scratched about for worms and dusted himself with sand, jerking his head back up comically–staring up at me for the laugh! Quite comical this bird: it was as if he wanted to entertain me! At the very least the bird was attempting to draw my attention. That much was certain.

"You're not going to believe this, Terry, but there's a huge white bird outside in my garden, and he's trying to make friends with me," I told my nurseryman friend, still following the bird's movements. "Now he's scratching for worms and then he comes back up, looking at me with a funny face, like he trying to get applause."

"Uh-huh, all right, whatever you say," my friend concluded, not wishing to follow the bizarre idea any farther. Finishing up business as quickly as I could, when I put down the phone, there was no longer a bird in view. Making for the side door, I stepped outside. There the bird stood, waiting for me! I got a better look now: This was no wild bird and this was no domesticated bird either. This was an exotic creature all right, beautiful to behold. The eyes! The bird has human eyes! Standing at about 4-ft-height, the swan-dove was the average height of a Trumpeter Swan, and yet, his bill was definitely *not* swan-like–it was dove-like! None of that really mattered when I looked again at his eyes: By the eyes I knew that I was in the presence of a spirit-bird.

Silently I began communicating with those big brown orbs–so full of warm compassion! My first instincts were to hug him, but I held back. Then it came to me that he might be here to soothe my heart from the shadows of my fantasy love affair. Naming my lover, I asked the bird if he had come to heal me from my pain as I was in agony at night, alone. The thought of jumping into the ocean had occurred to me, fantasizing death as a less painful alternative to life. My suffering was taking its toll on me–my secret lover keeping up a relentless pace so as not to lose the momentum of the fantasy chase. Apparently, my lover was not as sensitive; at times I felt near death.

So, when I asked the bird if he had come to help me through the pain, the graceful bird bowed his head low as if to say "Yes, I am here with you, to see you through." Again, I wanted so much to hug the big white bird but resisted the temptation.

"Tell him I love him," I said, to which the bird bowed his head low again. I looked long at the bird's human eyes, eyes so compassionate and loving–expressing a love so deep he gave me hope and peace and a thrill all at once. All I could muster was "You are so beautiful," to which the bird bowed a third, and last, time. We both saw my cat sauntering out the door, walking slowly in our direction. I looked at the bird and saw him thinking! Such human eyes! The bird was anticipating the actions necessary for takeoff–a difficult feat for such a large bird. I watched him take his first running steps down the long, sloping lawn–his running gear synchronized to his wingbeats. Generating just enough airflow for take off, rising up somewhat laboriously–Guinness and I watched the Swan-Dove become airborne, flying off to the south-southwest. Remarkable to see were the silver underlinings of his wings: Reflecting the sun each time his flight moved one span to the west, I saw that the timing of his flight pattern followed a musical tempo: *south south-west... south south-west... south south-west...*

One month later, I had a luncheon meeting in Paso Robles with a client from Silverado Trail in St. Helena. After a drive through sections of the vineyards recently purchased by his winery, we stopped at an outdoor bistro for a quick bite. A sudden windstorm hurled its force through the cafe, swiping away napkins and cutlery and whipping to the floor several glasses of Sauvignon blanc. Portents of a coming storm, we decided to call it a day. Walking me to my truck, Rick was the first to see the long, white feather lying on the ground at the driver's side. Examining it for a moment, he made a comment on what a miracle it was that the windstorm had not blown it away: Here, a pure white feather lay at my door.

"This must be for you" Rick said in his kind manner, offering the feather to me. Turning the feather over I saw the silver underlinings of the Swan-Dove. Driving away, the distinctive odor of bird permeated the air, filling my truck with the unique avian perfume. The next miracle lasted a long time: my truck remained strongly bird-scented for a full month. I have the long white feather still.

It was time to consider these unusual circumstances as natural stepping stones into a mystic future. I was now certain I was being watched over by invisible guardians, who offered me kindness at critical times when I suffered severe emotional strain. Deep down I knew I must help myself; the secret affair had left me unnaturally weak.

Chapter 26   Patañjali

One's body, O king, is one's car: the soul within is the driver and the
senses are its steeds.
Drawn by those excellent steeds–when well-trained,
he that is wise pleasantly performeth the journey of life and awake in peace.
The horses that are unbroken and incapable of being controlled
always lead an unskilful driver to destruction in the course of the journey;
so one's senses, unsubdued, lead only to destruction.

Mahabharata. Vidur Niti. The Wisdom of Vidura

Sitting in lotus position on a big green cushion, Guinness lay on my lap curled in a ball. Intrigued by the *Yoga Aphorisms of Patañjali*, I sat this evening relishing a copy of my Isherwood/ Prabhavananda translation. I had learned of Patañjali years ago through Yogananda, and now Patañjali's masterly work was like medicine–a condensed Kriya Yoga. Yogananda teaches us that Patañjali's work is the same Yoga as that extolled by Krishna in the Bhagavad Gita–even the same as that known to Jesus Christ, St John, St Paul and other initiates. It was most intriguing to find that Patañjali's work had hooked that superb wizard of the electricities: Nikola Tesla. Tesla's good friend, Henri Coanda–the inventor of the world's first jet-powered aircraft–remembers for us Tesla's thoughts on Patañjali, saying to his friend: "*The Yoga Sutras of Patañjali* is the most important book on Earth".

Tesla was also influenced by the Vedic teachings of Swami Vivekananda, the chief disciple of Ramakrishna. Speaking at Chicago's Parliament of the World's Religions in 1893, the indefatigable Vivekananda–the "cyclonic monk"–had sprinkled the Vedic word over the U.S., introducing eastern philosophy. Somewhat like a "John the Baptist" figure, Vivekananda prepared the western mind not long before Yogananda introduced Kriya Yoga here.

Vivekananda and Tesla were friends. Exposed to Vedic thought, Tesla observed the striking resemblance between the Vedic cosmological descriptions of matter and energy and that of modern physics. The electrical super-sage with an ultra-penetrating mind– Tesla was capable of grasping the abstruse cosmological concepts of the ancients, adopting Sanskrit words like *akasha* and *prana* into his lexicon, applying Vedic knowledge to his own observations of matter and energy force. Tesla clearly perceived the nature of the electrical substance that pervades the universe.

Vivekananda's explanations of Yoga are so clear:

'According to yoga philosophy, each soul is potentially divine. The goal is to manifest this Divinity within by controlling nature, external and internal... The Yogi claims that he who controls mind controls matter also. The internal nature is much higher than the external and much more difficult to grapple with, much more difficult to control. Therefore he who has conquered the internal nature controls the whole universe; it becomes his servant.'

To the western mind, the eastern concept of taking control of our internal nature–is no easy feat. Patañjali, in ancient times, devised methods leading the practitioner to success–called the eight "limbs" of Yoga. Merging ideas from various authors, my notes on the Yogic limbs read something like this:

1 - Yama: Purifying the mind by cultivating ethical virtues

2 - Niyama: Obtaining purity of body and mind by self-discipline

3 - Asana: Right posture, pleasing posture

4 - Pranayama: Control of prana–the life currents in the body, subtle, involuntary electricities

5 - Pratyahara: Withdrawal of the mind from sense objects; re-straint of the senses from their objects

6 - Dharana: Focused concentration on a point, or a chosen ideal

7 - Dhyana: Meditation; prolonged concentration—the power of flowing in an unbroken current

8 - Samadhi: The seedless state of Superconsciousness. Absorption in the Atman, the experience of the oneness of the individualized soul with Cosmic Spirit. Sphere of direct knowledge

Having reviewed the 8 limbs, I sat in lotus position to contemplate Patañjali's aphorisms. Everything was going well until "twenty-eight minutes and forty-eight seconds" into meditation: Something *BIG* had happened while meditating on an aphorism in the "*Powers*" section, which sutra reads: "*By making samyana on the heart, one gains knowledge of the contents of the mind.*"

Still intoxicating myself with delusions of my fantasy lover, I had experimented with this sutra—desperate to know the contents of mystery-man's heart. For the traveler who sets out alone, these Yogic *powers*—when applied outside the guidance of one's spiritual preceptor—can be very dangerous. The heart has a fiery electronic force. I was a child playing with fire, without "parental" guidance.

A "totem" of sorts added drama to the potency of this bizarre mystic experience: I had found in a second-hand store a framed silver-and-blue wine label, deciding to keep it as memorabilia as it denoted my mystery-lover's vineyard. The powder blue and silver glistening, the *totem* hung on the wall a few feet above my head as I sat in lotus posture contemplating the line on page 130. Setting the book down, I folded my hands together in meditation *mudra* and proceeded to make samyana on lover boy's heart. Internal process flowing, I reach the stage of *unbroken current*. Guinness was purring on my lap.

I reach the stage of prolonged concentration, approaching the stage when identical thought-waves arise in succession without interference from any other thought. My thought-current becomes one of near-perfect continuity. Reaching this plateau, my mind is perfectly one-pointed on one idea alone: lover boy's heart. Maintaining this uninterrupted state of consciousness for twenty-eight minutes and forty-eight seconds, I am absorbed into his heart, as I enter a low state of samadhi. In this lower octave, my thought-wave merges–affinitized with the current flowing in my third eye–the current of lover boy's heart. My thought-wave coincides with *lover boy's thought wave*, our mental vehicles now in resonance–the thought-currents in perfect rhythmic flow, vibrating in sympathetic currency. Entering into identical frequency, the electromagnetic valence forms a new circuitry, a dance of our merging thought-waves.

...I begin to hear the rumbling, a drum-like sound is gaining momentum. Tremors arise, thunderous. Earthquake sounds strike my ear, throwing me instantly out of samadhi. Guinness bolts. Raucous tremors shake the walls. Frightened, I search for signs of disaster–peering out the window for hints of an earthquake. It's too dark outside to see anything other than distant lights of the village below. The silver-blue frame! The *TOTEM*! I see the totem is rocking back and forth, threatening to fall from its mounting. I remove the silver-blue frame from the wall and immediately, simultaneously–peace takes over and the room is quiet again. It was the frame! The totem! Rushing outside I lay the silver-blue frame on the sandy ground, well away from the house. The tremors tone down precipitously, terminating in one final spasm.

I have opened Pandora's box! Fearful of the contents, I stand in the room–in psychological paralysis–terrified by the experience of the unleashing. I had indeed unsealed the private contents of his heart; now I stood stone-like, petrified. Peeking beyond the veil, a tidal wave had come rushing out–the veiled vision unveiled: My lover carried leather suitcases in his heart, the color of murky chartreuse; symbolic of jealousy. I had forced entry. I saw the sign. I was terrified.

Sitting in reflection, I thought over the experience: Now I understood why Christ spoke sharply against those who seek a sign. Having found the thread, I entered into the world of occult powers. I had witnessed the awesome potency of the powers–powers which I had used for selfish purposes. I shuddered to think of indiscriminate uses of these powers–occult powers in the wrong hands, of those practicing the dark arts who use the powers to harm others. I had learned a valuable lesson. Immediately I put the book out of reach. I would not open it again for years.

Proficiency in the occult powers is most definitely *not* a measure of one's spiritual attainment. Patañjali regards the occult powers as a stumbling block on the path to truth. Sri Ramakrishna refers to them as "Heaps of rubbish". Having experimented with the fiery toys, I came to see this sage wisdom firsthand. I left the fiery toys alone.

Chapter 27 Orange Blossom Special

The symbol of the spirit-knowledge is a flower.

The command can be communicated to the disciple from outside by a swift sending. Whereas, the spirit-knowledge blossoms from within, and cannot be evoked by any wand. Like a flower, the knowledge blooms in its destined hour.

El Morya

From my Faerie Fest gatherings, I had amassed a fair number of friends, Nell among them–famous for her role as *Queen of the Amazons*. Through Nell I met Jim, who had coached our *Midsummer Night's Dream* extravaganza. An iconic sort getting on in years–his huge *Yoda* ears made Jim an ideal cartoon character. When out of earshot, we referred to him affectionately as "Baba"– not an unusual name for someone who packed into storage his belongings every other year, escaping to India to join some new group of *sanyasi* pilgrims at the moments' ashram-du-jour. Highly amusing, Jim was well read and quite intelligent–when he wasn't stoned. Somewhat doddering and flaky, he was an ardent partaker of the herb.

Jim and I met up for one of Nell's parties, the *Queen of the Amazons* being famous for her Pismo Beach home entertainment center. When we arrived the beehive was already swarming. Artists and philosophers, scientists and activists, believers and skeptics—all types gelled in Nell's magnetic presence, drawn together in various discussions.

Jim whisked me expertly through the crowd. Being the habitual partaker–immediately he pawned me off on a very large woman I'd never seen before and, in his quickstep, left us to get his fix– the bobbing *Yoda* ears giving him away until he disappeared into the throngs. Settling in to the new environment, my eyes moved over to acknowledge the large woman sitting across the patio table. Somewhat taken aback by the sight of the heavily made up face and the bulging cheeks rouged ruby red–I saw that most of her lipstick had reserved a seat on the rim of her Champagne glass. Surely it must have been for entertainment value that Jim seated me here, I thought, finding myself involuntarily captive in the inordinately capable hands of this overweight glamor-puss, whose large bearing set my eyes to popping, once I got past the announcement of her garish cologne and sequins. Once beyond those obstacles I halted again–at the heavy-artillery of her traffic-stopping, size 50 dress and plumage–extravagant in the extreme–a reenactment of a turn-of-the-century MGM stage dancer perhaps? I was not surprised to learn "Chatanna" was a former stage actress, but it was unclear whether she had met with success. I surmised that her alarming capacity to move people around as she so willed must have been downright useful at one time–her 5 ex-husbands making a strong case. In glowing patois and stuffy self-approbation, the insensitive mass of a woman prattled on about her achievements.

Finding at length her soliloquy gaseous, her facade impermeable–the boasting machine left me no space to breathe or think, especially since I sat downwind of her hybrid stench of alcohol and cheap cologne, the nauseous mixture escaping through her ruby-lipped exhaust pipe. Perturbed, I thought to myself: 'All incoming traffic arriving at Chatanna Street intersection will be tied up for 5 hours due to an organic malfunction in the frozen-solid green light. All traffic advised to take detour'.

I decided to fix the malfunction myself: Raising my hand up to signal *YIELD* I followed up by feigning, in childlike urgency, my need for a potty pass–exiting summarily. Making a mental note to avoid that intersection, I escaped–meandering through the multitude, taking in the faces, races and styles–concluding that I was the youngest bird in the nest. Observing the thoughts and etiquette of those gathered, I thought of Nell's propitious grouping as a lodestone: a magnet shining with creative freethinkers, the atmosphere super charged with spirited debates. Over here was a didactic dart-meister throwing bulls-eyes and waxing philosophic. Over there bellows of righteous indignation circled the airwaves–something about "corp-pirates". Scanning the island of patio tables, I spotted a crew of serious heads, deliberating on US intelligence intrigues, hurriedly passing that table.

I placed a secret bet that I would not find one clear-minded group of heads in the wine-saturated quarter. Moving toward a spirited cluster–to my surprise–I happened upon an interesting discussion; philosophers lamenting the state of mankind's *Fall* from grace. I lost my secret bet: perhaps this table held some promise. Lingering a moment too long, a nice-looking gentleman insinuated himself at my left wing, introducing himself as "Caleb". Coveting a plan of escape, I was leaning towards heading home. Overdosed on social table rounds, I was rehearsing which exit card to play to Caleb's entrée, when the *unexpected* took possession of me: the scent of citrus spiced the air, the elemental *Sylphs* releasing a delicate anointment of *Hesperidian* orange-blossoms, thoroughly altering the atmosphere and suspending me between two worlds.

"Ah," I breathed dreamily, inhaling the special delivery,"To be or not to be among the living in these Elysian fields of California." It seemed an appropriate response to the Bard's phrase. "Perhaps Lord Bacon himself sent us the citrusy unguent," I added, not much concerned whether Caleb knew the connection.

Nothing compares to these rare gifts, the heaven-on-earth-moments when poetic bouquets from the world of the muses remind us to tarry awhile, *To be* in the moment. Recovering from my rutaceous rapture, I simply forgot to play my trump card and stayed on a while longer, enjoying the soirée. Held over by a timely vapor of *Orange Blossom Special*, I remained somewhat transfixed, dreamy–making my way alongside Caleb as he escorted me to a quiet overlook above the peridot-green waves, glistening in the moonlight. We spent some time comparing notes: As for the stage entrance of the citrine *phosphor* both of us were certain that we were the only ones sober enough to perceive the momentary grace. Waxing poetic the duration of the evening, lifted in gratitude to the sweet-smelling miracles of nature, I thought to myself:

"Breathe deeply into psyche O lovely flower blossoms

As thou would the essence of Heliotrope,

Remember always the true blue Forget-me-not!"

There was a more-than-ordinary force present that night when a spiritual breath seemed to sanction the *Rose Cottage*. Amidst the fragrant whisperings, Nell's home was a rare outpost. Her soirée seemed to reflect the drama of the green peridots christening the Pacific below.

Chapter 28 Tesla's Dove

Who then are My people?
Those who do not feel any place to be their home;
those who do not attach any value to objects;
who love to ascend mountains;
who love the singing of birds;

Inscribe upon the first stone A Dove;
upon the second A Warrior;
and upon the third A Pillar;
upon the fourth The Sun.

El Morya

Far from being ornithologists with "life lists," Nell and I were mad about birds, both of us "listing" original bird stories for our combined bird reliquary: I had my human-eyed *Swan-Dove* who bowed graciously three times and Nell had her doves, *Columba livia*, whom she patently refused to call pigeons. At one time she kept her doves caged in her garden–until prompted by what she sensed was a bird *oversoul*–a bird *Deva*. The *Deva* kept up a steady knocking at her conscience until Nell could no longer stand up to the guilt, letting free all her doves. As with most anyone who lingers in the presence of this modern-day Goddess, the doves returned to their keeper – on Valentine's Day – requesting from Nell re-adoption.

She had resident blue jays which, she said, laughing, "If we cared at all for snobbery we could correct everyone who errs, prompting their official title: *Scrub Jays*. As one Jay approached near us, we marveled at the rich turquoise beauty, agreeing the electric blue feathers deserve a more royal moniker.

Nell's wingspan was built like a big welcome sign; her miracle smile always ready to heal the forlorn guest. Never had I stood in the presence of one so nurturing: A wounded warbler–bird or human– could always find warmth at her *Rose Cottage*, a nurturing nest so full of compassion and encouragement. A Goddess in the flesh, the world sorely needed a skyway full of Nells.

The dove must have been listening: Straight down from the orange tree, she perched on the bronze statue of Kuan Yin, the resident deity.

"Jules. Did you know Nicola Tesla, the super-brain inventor, had a dove friend?"

"I trust a man who loves birds," I said, pulling oxalis deep at the root, weeding her tomato bed. "I loved reading *The Return of the Dove*."

"Amazing book. I just get so soft inside picturing him feeding that white dove during his lonely days in that hotel." Nell looked up at the sky. "Fixing that damn mess Edison made–Crikey, no one else on earth knew what to do. Retrofitting Edison's exploded mess from DC to AC in JP Morgan's shi-shi hotel..Imagine Tesla's pain... being an outcast, so alone in his hotel room for days and days. That dove never missed a day coming to his window, cooing for peanuts." Nell revivified my memory perfectly. We both looked up at the clouds gathering, blocking the sun.

"The dove came for Tesla's companionship too, don't you think? Don't you think that dove loved Tesla as much as the peanuts?"

"Maybe so. Tesla was as pure as that dove was white. What I do know is that Tesla ran circles around Edison," Nell said proudly.

"Making a pun? You know...alternating current goes around...? She missed it, going deeper in thought.

"Huh?...Anyway, material greed killed his inventions. Without Tesla, we're still floundering in the dark ages."

"Way ahead of his time," I agreed, wistfully. "I'll be right back. I'm getting on your computer to pull out your Tesla's quotes."

"Today's scientists have substituted mathematics for experiments, and they wander off through equation after equation, and eventually build a structure which has no relation to reality."

"The mind is sharper and keener in seclusion and uninterrupted solitude....Originality thrives in seclusion free of outside influences beating upon us to cripple the creative mind. Be alone, that is the secret of invention; be alone, that is where ideas are born."

Chapter 29   Little Alexandria

People are attracted by beauty and by luminous knowledge. Only that
Teaching which contains all hope, which makes life beautiful, which
manifests action, can promote true evolution. Certainly life is not
a market, where one can make a fine bargain for entrance into the
Heavenly Kingdom. Certainly life is not a grave, where one trembles
before the justice of an Unknown Judge!

El Morya

It was her library that enticed me to return, the literary treasures
that took possession of 3 contiguous rooms, a "*Little Alexandria.*"
Numbering just under a thousand volumes, absolutely zero books
would ever be checked out again, following the heartbreaking scene
worthy of a Sophoclean tragedy when one of Nell's finest treasures
never made the return trip up the Nile. Under the strict no-check
policy *Little Alexandria* saw quite a bit of me that summer.

Sampling a pool of philosopher's stones, I waded through waters
of Schopenhauer, Spinoza, Krishnamurti, Descartes, Leibniz,
Berkeley, Kant, Hegel, Goethe and Watts. Passing through deep
rivers of Rudolf Steiner's mind, I found his mystical gates beyond
my capabilities. I met Theodore Fechner, the "father of the new
psychology" of the 1800s—one of Nell's favorites, herself a psych
professor. From Alpha to Omega, crossing the threshold into *Little
Alexandria* one felt as though entering an *Egyptian Hall of Learning*.

I hurried off one weekend to the literary shrine to find Nell
upstairs, whisking her blond locks from her milky-white skin.
In her easygoing manner and sultry, Texas-breezeway voice she
directed half a dozen contractors in the line of duty. Among the
help, I counted a mumbling plumber, 3 masons and her Costa
Rican builder-friend who was visiting for the summer. Behind
them all slumped the meek Mike, a luckless carpenter waiting his
turn, his torso fixed in worshipful obeisance toward his Goddess-

like employer. Picking up a call from her cell, Nell finally noticed me at the secret stairs. Smiling and waving, I escaped the throng of hammer-and-wrench-wielding workmen and followed the steps down to the lower level. Winding around a golden Buddha statue I stopped just long enough to enjoy a moment of mirth, greeting last years' faded Christmas decorations adorning the breezeway. I let myself inside one of two separate cottages and exhaled deeply. I had entered the sacred space of *Little Alexandria*, off-limits to all but Nell's inner circle.

Boiling water for a cup of tea, I could not stop thinking about the tall, blonde dynamo upstairs. On top of her hectic vacation rental business, Nell was now consumed in the effort to save the coast: The State Off-Highway Vehicle Division had turned Oceano Dunes into a destruction zone–the cause of a rising annual mortality rate, a dangerous air pollution health hazard and not least, an ecological disaster affecting untold wildlife.

How did she balance such an energy expense account? Factoring in her love of the sauce and a haphazard diet, where was her energy coming from and how did she keep her sanity amidst such an unrelenting pace? Besieged with constant inquiries and contracts, she was still fresh, hosting guests from around the world, and managing it all with the alacrity of a tree-swinging monkey.

She must be inspired, I mused. Yes, she was a model of *inspired humanity*, moved to do what is right, her horsepower spurred by a sense of liberty and justice for all. Having answered my own question satisfactorily, I settled into a big chair with a big cup of peppermint tea to pick up where I had left off: Immanuel Kant.

"Your books are simply scrumptious, Nelly," I chirped, meeting the blonde dynamo at the top of the secret stairs just before sunset. The secret stairwell connected the sprawling upstairs/ downstairs of the *Rose Cottage*, which was an outpouring of 5 private dwellings built in inspired stages over time–a curious amalgamation of egress/ ingress such that a newbie could easily get lost in the options. Only her inner circle used the secret stairwell, which was hidden behind closed doors.

"I'll be right back Jules. Join me upstairs. I'm going to grab some wine from the cellar."

I headed downstairs, outside to her now-famous *Orange Blossom Special* tree. Choosing a few beauties, I returned upstairs to the kitchen to prepare some vegetables I'd brought from my garden. Reared in the school of *fresh everything*, nutrition was always foremost in my mind. Processed food was, as my Dad would say: *Pizon*.

"Whose head are you looking into now?" Nell expertly opened a 750ml bottle of Charles Krug Merlot.

"I'm having a love affair with Immanuel Kant, even though I can't seem to get my head around his. I am hoping *something* will stick."

"It's all good, Jules, it's all for the good. I had a crush on Kant too." Nell broke into a southern-smooth mischievous smile. "Just keep on it, dream on it–and see what comes of it. Jules, Jules... *Jules*! Have you read *Blavatsky*?" Nell's eyes shone like a harbinger of epiphany.

"Not yet. I tried her some years back but I was too unripe for such exalted heights."

"Honey-pie, *Blavatsky* is a Russian *Jhansi Ki Rani*! You *must* try her again. Excuse me, someone's at the door." Nell returned to the table with a tall gentleman in his 50s.

"Jules, I want you to meet Philo, our very dear friend whom we all adore. Philo's a photographer, creates amazing art. Plus, he's my personal savior–helps me fix *everything* around here." Nell was purring as she poured Philo a glass of Merlot. The benign gentleman took a seat, joining our petit repast.

"Philo, we were just talking about Blavatsky. Jules hasn't read her yet."

"Unfortunately for mankind, spiritual-warrior-humanists like HPB are very rare." Philo spoke slowly, studying well his own thoughts.

"Few there are willing to sacrifice themselves for humanity," Philo added solemnly.

Admonishing myself for my literary deficiencies, I couldn't help feeling utterly inadequate. I could not participate in their discussion. Botany had not prepared me for the intellectual milieu of the Rose Cottage.

"Philo, tell Jules about Blavatsky's role in metaphysics," Nell urged her placid guest.

"That is Adrian's bailiwick. What I *can* say is that her triumphs are in her books, appreciated much more now than in her time. Scholar that she was, HPB's writings introduced humanity to the initiatic path, to a higher level of consciousness. She did her best to help humanity understand the ultimate goal."

"The ultimate goal?" I asked, trying to follow Philo's track.

"The goal? The *goal* is the path of initiation, penetrating the ancient mysteries—the science of the Self—the *One Self in all Selves*...I believe that is how she puts it."

I didn't dare interrupt the kind man, even though I had questions. Nell vanished momentarily to locate Blavatsky' writings.

"Mankind is on the threshold of a very bright phase in the endless cycles of evolution," Philo continued. "A Blavatsky is a rare gem: Not many have both the brains *and* moxie to plunge the depths of esoteric teachings. When the day arrives that western science links with eastern philosophy—only when that link is forged will we see science progress. So long as modern materialism continues to suppress true innovation—we will not see any *real* progress. Materialism kills original innovation".

Returning with two large books and a stack of rumpled notes, Nell took the floor. "Listen to Blavatsky:

The existence of God and immortality of man's spirit may be demonstrated like a problem of Euclid. The Oriental philosophy has room for no other faith than an absolute and immovable faith in the omnipotence of man's own immortal self. This omnipotence comes from the kinship of man's spirit with the Universal Soul–God!'"

"Madame is speaking of the Universal Soul–or "God" as *Anima Mundi*–the great mover and shaker," Philo agreed. "The ancients have spoken of Universal Soul for thousands of years–so far beyond what modern science today dares to imagine. Why? Because the ancients were initiated into the *true* arts and sciences! They perceived phenomena with their superconscious sight, saw everything linked to the one *Akashic* substance–*Akas*, the cosmological hologram. Everything in the universe is but a division from the *one* radiant substance. Everything that exists is nothing but a mere *idea*, originating from the one primordial source, infinitely dividing itself. What we see subjectively is only an inference, insubstantial–a chimera."

"That's deep Philo, not exactly an easy concept to get the head around. Everything is merely an *idea* originating from universal light substance?" I had come across these concepts before, never putting them on the front burner. Hearing them now, I made a mental sticky note for my next visit to *Little Alexandria*.

"Oh, how I love that woman," Nell chirped, refilling Philo's glass with the non-potable red liquid. Running her fingers through the pages of *Isis Unveiled*, she stopped at an index. "Madame was a spiritual warrior par excellence. Listen to her:

'Between these two conflicting Titans–Science and Theology–is a bewildered public, fast losing all belief in man's personal immortality, in a deity of any kind, and rapidly descending to the level of a mere animal existence. Such is the picture of the hour, illumined by the bright noonday sun of this Christian and scientific era!'"

"Things haven't changed much since then," I lamented. Hearing the power behind the writer's thoughts, I felt Madame's spirit calling. I was wishing I had been there with her.

"Blavatsky left a huge, indelible footprint," Philo said, sipping his wine. "Sacrificed herself as a kind of litmus test–probing humanity's readiness. They weren't ready in the late 1800s and they aren't quite ready still. Since Einstein, we have not seen much real progress in physics, still floundering in a patchwork of hazy, inferential theories."

"Perceptions of higher truths lie *beyond* time and space. Western science doesn't have the moxie to go there–except by inferences." Nell downed her glass of red rotgut, the Merlot just beginning to show its influence.

"Blavatsky's teachers followed the doctrines of Buddha," Philo continued, jumping the track a bit. "The mind must be emptied. *White Space* is the requirement for perceiving the lofty dimensions."

I detected ethanol's influence, noticing Philo's slight slurring. I knew these slips to be signs heralding my impending exit. "I know something about *White Space*," I said, cheerfully. "I make *White Space* every time I meditate–divorcing myself completely from body consciousness."

"I'm afraid meditation is not my thing," Nell admitted. "I can't sit still long enough."

"Blavatsky had natural abilities in *White Space*," Philo said, moving the topic a bit, perhaps sidestepping the subject of meditation.

"Before I go, please oblige me a paltry botanical metaphor," I said, getting up from the table. "From what I've heard this evening, it seems to me that humanity's evolutionary fruit appears to be rotting beneath thick weeds of materialism. If materialism occludes the ancient wisdom from reaching us, then modern science cannot procure proper seeds for the future. An ecologist would say man's evolution is rotting in an early seral stage. If an ecologist were to assess man's ecological future, they might recommend burning the material rubbish, starting innovations fresh on virgin soil–thereby letting in the sun and allowing young sprouts the opportunity to mature into a global forest. From what you say, it seems to me that if we fail to link science to the ancient teachings—humanity will never mature as a species into a *climax community*."

"Oh, Jules, I just love your little plant ways." Nell said sweetly, the implications of the Merlot taking over.

Bidding farewell, I excused myself to be alone with my thoughts. Driving home along the quiet streets of Pismo, the veil of summer fog played visual tricks. Passing through the town, the Doppler effect was in evidence, changing the halo-tones around the bright city lights upon approach. Had I been proficient in math and physics, I would have tried to devise meaningful applications through the art of trigonometry, offering them to the science. I would have loved the challenge of linking the science of Kriya Yoga with art. In my meditations I saw how matrices and lattices described time and space warps. Coming up on the familiar *Cypress* and *Eucalyptus* hedgerows sheltering Arroyo Grande Valley, I imagined the towering wind-blown crowns in a dramatic image: as gesticulating sine waves of a thousand cheering hands, moving ecstatically across a giant stadium.

Chapter 30 My Spiritual Preceptor

*The mind which follows the rambling senses,
makes the Soul as helpless as the boat which
the wind leads astray upon the waters.*

Bhagavad Gita II.70

Pulling from Nell's library shelves *The Secret Doctrine*, I asked myself: Do I really have the energy at this late hour to attempt such labyrinthine syntax? Trying a few years ago to follow the mind of *Helena Petrovska Blavatsky* proved so daunting, I gave up after the second chapter. What made me think I could do any better now, at 11:00 p.m.?

HPB, the scholar-mystic, absolutely fascinated me–the multilingual Ukrainian Countess ranking as modern history's most accomplished and profound amanuensis. Writing *Isis Unveiled, The Secret Doctrine, The Voice of the Silence* and volumes of letters, articles and translations of ancient Tibetan texts–she founded *The Theosophical Society*–with outposts in America, England and the Indian subcontinent. Not without her peccadilloes, the bold lioness painted for posterity an immortal picture of the cosmos. Her contributions to our knowledge of ancient, esoteric cosmology left a lasting impression; her character impossible to forget.

I had a growing desire to visit Tibet. Knowing her teachers lived there, I conjured up images of the snowy fastnesses in the Himalayan heights which, ever since my early days of Kriya Yoga, had held a soft spot in my heart. Imagining I was traveling to Tibet with Madame was a pleasing image as I took her book on my lap once more.

Damn! If only I had that woman's grey matter. Alas, I was better suited for forests and flowers. Failing again, I was reluctant to return the volume to the shelf. Frustrated, I could not read HPB but neither could I now sleep. Wide awake from the opening pages of *The Secret Doctrine*, I was mentally functioning somewhere in the temples high in the northern wilderness. Switching gears, I pulled from the shelf Madame's tiny book of *Golden Precepts,* a gem which she translated from Sanskrit and renamed *The Voice of the Silence*. I began reading her introduction:

'The work forms part of the same series as that from which the 'Stanzas' of the Book of Dzyan were taken, on which the Secret Doctrine is based. Together with the Paramartha, which, the legend of Nagarjuna tells us, was delivered to the great Arhat by the Nagas or 'Serpents' (in truth the name given to the ancient Initiates), the 'Book of the Golden Precepts' (Voice of the Silence) claims the same origin.'

She goes on to say these Precepts are found in Krishna's teaching to Arjuna and again in the *Upanishads*. I followed Madame through the first door, *The Hall of Learning*. By the time I had reached *The Hall of Wisdom* it was midnight and my eyes were blood red. There was nothing left of my brain with which to absorb the concentrated precision of her *Precepts*. When at last my eyes shut down for the night, I remember clasping Madame's *Voice of the Silence* to my heart, like precious cargo. With her book close beside me, I dozed off into the night voyage ahead. To the stars with Madame!

Six a.m. next morning the book was nowhere in sight! Searching under the sheets and pillows—no luck. Surely Madame could not just disappear in thin air. To avoid the approaching panic, I tried bringing up the levitating lines of Tommy Lee Jones' directive: 'Search every farmhouse, henhouse, outhouse, doghouse...' The laughing medicine worked. Regaining a semblance of calm, I retraced the entire bed and under the bed. Coming up empty, I tasted the first epinephrine molecule. In the blur of 6 a.m. logic, my puny brain could think of nothing else but Nell's precious library book. Had an awful fate come to Madame's volume? *Shiza*!

Pausing briefly, attempting to clear the mental fog—I slumped down on the bed, holding my head between the palms of my hands, but failed to muster anything useful. Except one thought: Water. Walking briskly around the California King, making ready to grab my glass from the bedside table–I saw it. What the...? What is *this* book doing here?–a good question, considering the fact that the paperback before my eyes was *not* present the night before. Even in the haze of dawn there was no doubt: I *knew* that my water glass was the *only* article on that table at midnight. Still half asleep, I picked up the book for a careful examination. It's spine was hanging by threads, pages were torn out–all of that inconsequential as the book now began to glisten, becoming somehow animated–as a lover would beam at the approach of his beloved. I studied the cover. Staring at the Statue of David with four colors crowning his brain, I read the title: *Studies of the Human Aura*. Turning it over, the biographical sketch read like a mystery: the author was a Hindu adept living his last years in Tibet. His name was "Kuthumi".

Within moments my body begins acting strange, sending me signals. Following his track, I attune to his ideas, to his mind. I lose touch with myself, eagerly drinking in the gems of new thought processes. By the time I finish the first page I am already somewhere outside of my body–which is vibrating. Now into the third page, I cannot take my eyes away from this voice. The author's thoughts are touching me deeply. I must not lose contact with this awesome connection. I am falling–with ease–into a strangely familiar psyche, into the soul of a mind so potent. Body becomes aware. Mind becomes aware. Soul interpenetration. I read on, very slowly. I desire to miss no thing. No word escapes me. My normal brain processes no longer in control, the substance of his soul spills into my being in waves, cleansing waves, sine waves, exhilarating waves. I am vibrating now in perfect sympathy with his soul, his frequency. This mind is *my* mind. This voice *belongs* to me, it is functioning in synchronous time, in perfect rhythm with my heart.

The gnosis instantaneous, visceral–for the first time in my life I *know*. Beyond all doubt I am holding in my hands a voice of wisdom. It is the first voice I have ever known to speak *directly* to my inner being, my *Real Self*. At long last the still, small voice inside me recognizes the words of my spiritual preceptor, my guru.

Never before had the stillness said so much. Through the *Voice of the Silence*, I could hear my Teacher calling me home. Clutching the book as a prized possession, I could not let the precious teacher out of my grasp, nor lift my eyes from his pages.

Chapter 31 Comanche in Ponytails

"Jules, there's someone I want you to meet!" Nell yelled from the upstairs balcony, tossing me instantly off my cloud.

"Be right up," I reacted mindlessly, only semi-aware of my words. Pulling on my yellow jacket, I entered the back garden, bowing to Kwan Yin seated in all her morning glory. Plucking a small stem from the fragrant *Orange Bergamot*, I rounded the brick path to touch the statue of St.Francis.

Ascending the stairway breathing the fumes of my nosegay, I stopped. Through the open blinds of the western window I beheld a middle-aged Indian woman dressed in a long, red catholic-schoolgirl plaid skirt, shod in orthopedic Mary Jane shoes! The hair was parted in two very long brown pigtails, each of them tied with small red-and-white ribbons, looking much like a Christmas gift all wrapped up. As she tossed a pigtail behind her, I noticed the oversized wooden cross hanging from her neck by a black leather lanyard. Entering through the door, I approached the Indian maiden.

"Jules, darlin', meet Adrian, my personal angel savior. She's here to clean. Cleans all my cottages. I would be dead without her. When she goes, I go!"

"So nice to meet you, Adrian. Pardon me but you don't look the part. You look more like an Indian maiden. Nell speaks so highly of you, calls you a priestess."

"Come, let us sit," Nell said, sensing a special meeting was at hand.

"If you don't mind me asking, Adrian, how is it that you and Nell first met?" I tried to play down my intense curiosity. Taking her sweet time, Adrian dawdled, breathing the fresh brewed French Blend. I could see these two were in no hurry.

"Well, I worked for years waitin' tables in Pismo. Served Nell dinner for years at the place. She tipped me real big. About 10 years ago my cough was gettin' pretty bad. They fired me, said it wasn't good PR for the customers."

"That's when *I* got her!" Nell filled in the story, her eyes twinkling. "And I won't *ever* let her go!" Sitting between these two friends, I felt a warm current circulating. Deep respect over many years had joined them inextricably, the bond strength between them inseparable. I had evidenced Nell's remarkable magnetism, drawing clusters of fans. I was about to discover "Club Adrian".

"So," I urged, impatiently," please continue Adrian, I'm dying to hear more."

"Hold tight there, honey, I'm not as young as you. Just let me enjoy my fresh coffee here. You just sit a spell and relax. You'll hear everything your little heart wants to know."

Obediently, I settled back down in my chair, trying to adjust to the slower, Texan pace. It was apparent the Indian maid preferred *legato*. Gently admonished, I was about to learn some lessons in southern etiquette, taking solace in the fact that I was lucky to be one among this triad. I became fascinated by Adrian's individuality; her quiet confidence astounded me.

"I was raised in a little town outside Houston, a few hundred miles from Nell, but we didn't know each other then...and, well, I'm a wee bit older than this young chickadee here," she said, flipping a pigtail, finally indulging me. "My Mama was only 14 years young when she got pregnant with me, and back then–'specially in them red-neck woods–whoa! My Mama would'a been shamed first and maybe shot after that for gettin' knocked up by an Indian boy," she said, smirking, letting us know we were headed for some theater. "Yup, full-blooded Indian boy, not much older than my Mama. She got fat with a half-breed, movin' around in her belly. Yep, that would be me!"

I looked at Nell to get some kind of context. Was Adrian messing with me or was she for real? Finding Nell's eyes glued with affection for the Indian maid, I had my answer. This was the real Adrian, not a fibbing bone in her body, but one heck of a lot of actress. I returned my attention to the performance.

"Half-breeds aren't half welcome in Texas, not welcome at all in those days, not one bit welcome. Come to think about it, hasn't changed much. Necks still red as ever. Not much above them necks, neither! Ain't likely anything good ever's gonna come outa that place 'cept of course, me and Nell!"

Adrian paused, topping up her coffee mug. Nell was squirming, delighted to hear the story for the umpteenth time. Like a warm Texas wind, her voice just blew me away. I could feel Adrian stirring–she was warming up. The pigtailed comic had only just begun.

"So, when I was 3 weeks old, they put me in a reed basket just like Moses," the maid stated flatly, shifting forward, enlisting my full attention. "But, they didn't put me in no river–like they did Moses. No, took me to some rich folks' mansion." Adrian halted, taking a slow swig of caffeine. "They rang the doorbell and set me down on the doorstep, under the awning. Yep, they left me there in a reed basket, just like Moses."

"My God, Adrian!"I gasped. "But...so...what happened to you? Did they wait till someone answered the door? Did they just ring and leave, please go on."

"Hold your horses, Missy. Calm down," Adrian admonished me again. Unlike Texans, I was uncomfortable waiting through the long intermissions. I could barely manage to stay seated through the maid's slow, steady pacing. She looked over at Nell, who was smiling placidly, adoring her friend's dramatics, loving the way she drew it out, stretching the story along a long, curious road. Flipping her braids again, Adrian continued. "My Mama and her Indian-boy-lover hid behind the barn and watched and waited.

After some time, the butler answered the door. Yep, he saw me lyin' there in the basket, all tucked in with pretty pink blankets, right there where they left me. The nice butler picked up the basket with me in it and brought me inside to the Missus."

"Incredible!" I ejaculated. "So did they, I mean...the people living in that mansion–did they adopt you?"

"Nope,"Adrian replied flatly, taking a moment to rest, building the suspense. Taking a long swig off her mug, she paused to look at Nell. Swinging her pigtail again, she took up where she had left off. "Nope, the rich folks took me to *another* couple, some even richer folks who was wantin' a little baby girl."

"Wow! Unbelievable, Adrian, so then you lived happily ever after? I mean, your new parents, being of the gentry and all, they didn't mind that you were half Indian?"

"I guess my skin didn't look so dark to them! Bein' half-breed, well, that would'a been a sore embarrassment to my new Mama, haulin' me all over town makin' peoples' eyebrows raise up. My Mama always kept me in a pretty red bonnet and kept me outa the sun. She would'a figured out some kinda story, she was full that proper talk. I'm sure she told 'em lots of fibs, like I was a Princess from somewhere unknown. Would'a been just like her. My Mama could sure spin a yarn when she needed to."

"I've never heard anything like this, Adrian, and you seem to be so grounded and happy, in spite of such a traumatic beginning." I was admiring the survivor next to me, noting her strength, her bold presence.

Standing up suddenly, Adrian spread those unforgettable Mary Jane shoes wide apart on the floor, putting her hands on her hips. Squinting, looking the part of a gun-slinging Annie Oakley, she declared: "Now don't tell *me* I don't have no abandonment issues!"

I got up to relieve myself, leaving Nell in spasms. Returning to my seat, it dawned on me that Adrian's story was far from over.

What had become of her adoptive, gentrified parents that she now cleaned Nell's houses? What about her inheritance? Nell must have been reading my mind.

"Jules, can you believe it? Her Mama was so jealous of Adrian. After her Papa died, that woman turned her nose up at Adrian and pissed off her entire inheritance."

"Heartless bitch!" I exploded, managing to control stronger words floating as possibilities.

"Yep, she did. She just pissed it all off, but I didn't care about the money anyway. It was not worth having to deal with someone like that. After Daddy died she turned. I hardly recognized her anymore. Impossible to be around her. Christ! That woman could drive a herd of cattle away. No, I wanted to get free of the harpy's talons– grabbin' atcha when you weren't watchin'. That's when I moved to California. Everybody was much happier after that."

"So, what made her so jealous that she disinherited you?" Getting impatient again, I wanted to go straight to the heart of the saga.

"Well, my Daddy was a Shriner, see. You know, a member of the secret society of Freemasons." Before Adrian, I knew nothing at all of the Shriners. Reading later of the Ancient Arabic Order of the Nobles of the Mystic Shrine, I learned they were established in 1870 as an appendant body to Freemasonry and based in the United States.

"They're the ones wearin' red fezzes." Adrian was looking to see if I was following her. "The Shriner laws command them to silence, forbid members to divulge any secrets of Freemasonry. No lenience at all. Been that way ever since the days of Egypt, which is where it all came from originally. But I couldn't stand it, I wanted to know what my Daddy was doin', dammit! I deserved to know! One way or the other I was gonna find out his secrets. Wanted real bad to know 'em, but my Daddy refused."

We watched Adrian demonstrate how to dig a tunnel through to a father's heart. Standing up, crying "crocodile tears", she put on her best "poor little girl" face, begetting the most miserable pout, it made me want to reach out to console her. She was *that* good an actress.

"I would come to him beggin' in tears, big baby tears, like this, bigger and bigger till my Daddy's heart would be set to breakin' and it finally did! This act of mine eventually paid off–little by little, it did. I'd put on my innocent face and then I'd ask my Daddy just one simple question about the Freemasons, and tell him I just wanted one teeny bit. Well–inch by inch, I broke down his barriers. Took a *long* time though 'cuz he was such a good and loyal man, he really didn't wanna break his oath to the Shriners. So I just kept it up, with my sad little eyes and my pretty red dress on, looking like a good little Daddy's girl. Finally he broke down and said, OK, listen up, now Adrian. I cannot break my oath, but if you can look at my eyes, and understand my thoughts from your eyes–well, then you can have your answers. And that was how my Daddy taught me: silently, from his eyes. That's how I learned the secret teachings of Freemasonry. I'd just stare at him for a long time, while he gave me the Egyptian secrets through his eyes."

"You actually received his messages?" I inquired, half-believing her.

"Heck, yeah! Found out everything I needed to know!"

"Fascinating. What was it that made your Mother jealous?"

"Well," smiled Adrian, curling her mouth up mischievously, squirming in her chair, preparing herself. "You see, he didn't look in Mama's eyes near as long as he did mine!"

Nell stifled a giggle, not at the sad pathos of the story but at the caricature that only Adrian, in her catholic-girl-Indian-Princess style could possibly fit.

"So tell me," I asked, urging Adrian along again, "how did you manage so many years living with such tension? I mean while your Dad was still alive?"

"She sent me off to Grandpa's farm every summer, all summer long." Adrian eyes were twinkling, hinting at something more to come.

"Well, that was convenient of her," I spat out, in judgement. "Did you look forward to summertime?" I watched Adrian preparing for her next theatrical installment.

"Hell yes! I loved it. Had my own pony, named "Susie". We played dollies and dress up together. Used to put makeup on her, used to make her up *real* pretty."

"Oh, come on, Adrian, you're exaggerating. *Right?*"

"Even curled her eyelashes and put on mascara. Like I said, she looked *real* pretty."

"Come on, Adrian, you're playing with my head!" Having had a horse of my own, I was not going in for the comedienne's horse business. I never could submit to an eyelash curler and couldn't imagine a horse submitting to one.

"Nope, not joking. It's the truth."

"What? Shiza! Adrian, come on. What horse would allow their eyelashes to be curled?" I pushed Adrian hard, at the same time watching Nell closely, looking for a character witness. To my astonishment, Adrian was indeed telling the whole truth and nothing but the truth.

"I was real careful." Adrian became suddenly serious. "All except one time when I got hasty. Susie let loose on me, right here." Adrian lifted her skirt just above the knee, showing an old scar. "I never could run so good after that."

I decided to just go with it. Trust it. This Indian Princess was proving to be a story unto herself. Adrian had the stuff legends are made of.

"Jules, Adrian has an extensive metaphysical library and she lives just south of you, on Los Berros." Nell said in a loud whisper, well knowing my hunger for knowledge.

"Really! When can I visit? I mean..."

"Honey, you're welcome anytime. A friend of Nell's is a friend of mine. I'm no scholar, I'm a Comanche half-breed! But I sure know my metaphysics and I'd love to share with you everything I know. We'll do some ground work first and move to the sky when you're ready. Jesus is my guru." Adrian smiled, taking her huge wooden cross in a firm grasp. "Please, do come for a visit, darlin'. Anytime."

"Thank you, I would love to."

"Nell tells me you're reading Blavatsky."

"I *tried* reading her last night, but got lost in the esoteric hall of mirrors."

"The *unseen* is the greatest damn laboratory, honey. Been tellin' Nell that for years, but for some silly reason the invisible stuff scares her half to death."

"That's why I went into psychology, Adrian, to help people understand what they can't see." Nell deflected from Adrian's point.

"We're not talkin' about Freud here Nell," Adrian corrected her friend smartly. For the first time I saw a tiny flaw in my heroine, Nell–the flaw of fear. "Jules, did Nell tell you of her University days teaching psychology? She led a class-action suit for women's equal pay. Made her pretty unpopular when she beat 'em. When those jackals bared their fangs, she moved into real estate."

"You've got huevos, girl, going out on the front lines like that." I saluted Nell.

"Made me feel a little guilty for leaving after we'd won," Nell admitted.

"Fuck guilt!" The unexpected boom shot like a cannon straight from Adrian's mouth. It was her dramatic exit line. Adrian left us to begin her cleaning routine.

"Nell, I need to ask you about this book," I said, cornering her before she changed gears. I had carried the mysteriously-appearing book downstairs. Now I held it up to Nell. "Is this your book? I found it on the bedside table this morning. Did you put it there last night when I was asleep?"

"I have never seen this book before," she said, leafing through the pages. "No, this is definitely not my book."

"Did anyone come downstairs last night? Did you have any late visitors?"

"No one came. No, this is a mystery."

"Nell, that book was *not* on the bed-side table before I dozed off. I know that for sure. Are you *positive* this is not your book?"

"Let me look again," she said, taking the book back, going through the torn pages. "O, my God Jules! This has Caleb's writing in it! Oh, my God! Caleb's been dead for years. All his belongings are in the attic, locked up, inaccessible. No one goes up there. O Jules!"

"You haven't mentioned Caleb. Strange to say, that was the name of a fellow I met at your party. I was about to go home, but then we suddenly had a mystical experience from your orange tree– Oh, never mind that. What do you make of this book's sudden appearance?"

"Honey, I've got goosebumps. I have never seen that book before and I know *every* book that sits in my library."

"Nell, I have to ask you a favor. I cannot be without this book. It is calling to me. I know this is against your policy, but please, may I take it home to read?"

"Gosh, Jules, I don't know just this minute. It's all so sudden. I can't think straight. Read it here for the time being. I need to look at it again when I have time, and then we'll talk again."

Chapter 32   Comanche Medicine

Often through illness the achievements become intensified.
St. Francis and St. Theresa were often ill.
Pythagoras had heart disease.
The best zurnas often lacked some strings.

El Morya

"Good morning Adrian," I said, strolling through the semi-domesticated wilderness, approaching the pigtailed Comanche standing under the Spanish portico. Entering the grounds she called home for 30 years, I was always waylaid by the profusion of artistic freedom. Signs of Adrian were everywhere, hidden beneath the overgrowth of vines and timeworn pottery. Inhaling the perfume of scented geraniums and pink jasmine, the garden begged me to linger awhile. I was happy to see yellow and bronze nasturtiums skillfully competing for life at the edge of the greensward, beyond which an expanse of crabgrass held sway. Looking up 50 feet in the air at the mid-garden centerpiece– Tree of Heaven, *Ailanthus altissima*–the Chinese native provided shade for a patch of bright coral Impatiens. A Filipino fieldworker was tying up his snow peas in the plantation adjoining Adrian's acreage. Admiring the succulent pods hanging on blue-green rows, I was seized by a desire to hop the wire fence–dreaming for a hot second the smiling Asian might offer me a sampling of the crunchy legumes. It had been some years since my days as a "pesticide cop," but I never lost the compulsion to administer advice–like a Jewish mother–warning innocent fieldworkers of the toxic substances they were handling.

Seeing Adrian had gone back inside, I quickened my pace. Courteous students don't keep the teacher waiting. For some, Adrian provided a loving psychological assessment; for others she replenished a lost confidence. All who came to her table were searching after truth, a higher truth which could not be found in a world seething with New Age "avatars" barking up some exclusive magical fix–offered for a price. Adrian was different. Adrian was authentic, offering freely to all what she knew–from personal experience over seven decades of living–to be truth. She was a mystic who, like me, could hear messages through the currents.

Her philosophy held that her "pilgrims would progress" only after a thorough search inside themselves. Lenient in most other ways–on this point she stood like a *Comanche Elder,* responsible for all pilgrims on her reservation. She did not brook excuses. At this impasse, those failing this critical step were chastised–the Comanche illuminating their self-delusions, pointing the problem out theatrically, saying things like: 'You are lying to yourself. No one but you can deny yourself the truth. Do you want to continue fighting against your soul?' Students found in the state of denial were required to proceed to the next phase, to what she called her *Atlantean Mirror.* Holding up to our eyes a small looking glass, Adrian required us to speak to the image in the glass, to pour out our griefs–to remove once and for all the illusions setting us apart from our soul freedom. 'Now, look into this mirror again and talk to yourself. Tell yourself the truth!' She repeated the mirror exercise as many times as necessary.

Still somewhat bothered by my fantasy lover, I was not excluded from the *Atlantean* self-mirroring exercise. My forbidden fantasy-lover-boy's tentacles intermittently extended their reach, catching my attention when I least expected–occasionally hurling my spiritual progress backwards. I was addicted to the lie. That lie *had* to die before I could truly live and Adrian was just the person to help me live again. Through painful, honest self-examination, I trusted her psychological do-it-yourself treatment. It worked. In this style of confession, I was in full control, acting the part of both priest and confessioner. It did not take long to appreciate the enormous practicality of Adrian's ways and means, given lovingly to all pilgrims coming to her table.

Taking a seat at the huge oak table in her sun-drenched kitchen, I was only one among many fortunate pilgrims to have found her. Pouring me a cup of fresh coffee, she had me slice oranges from her citrus grove. Joining her hand in mine, she made a beautiful prayer in the name of Jesus, her chosen teacher—asking his personal blessing that this meeting bring peace and prosperity, not only to the two of us but for the *Universal Great All.* The profundity of her message and the base tones coming from deep within her heart emerged like great pipes of a church organ—ringing my heart and forcing tears to erupt unexpectedly from my eyes.

Adrian excused herself, returning with books from her library. Going through each book, she began the process of ascertaining both my knowledge and my proclivities. The only book that I had read was *The Return of the Dove*, both of us revering the gentle Nicola Tesla. Knowing I was a botanist preferring natural science to dry philosophy, she suggested I read *The Ancient Secret of The Flower of Life Vol.II*, by Drunvalo Melchizedek, dubbing it the kingpin that brought into mainstream knowledge such natural phenomena as Fibonacci spirals, the Golden Mean and the Platonic solids. Adrian and Drunvalo had been among the 144 making a pilgrimage to Merida, Mexico for a special ceremony conducted under a Mayan "Daykeeper" named Humbatzmen, a respected elder with deep knowledge of the Mayan calendar.

I was fascinated by her account of how Drunvalo, a pioneer in unconventional physics had, together with an electronics wizard, devised a method to remove toxic particles from the air. Using a vibrational technique similar to that used by Vedic sages, Drunvalo and his wizard friend tuned their device to a specific frequency using only *thought force.* Once their tuning was perfectly set, the sound waves themselves worked their wonders—dissipating a noxious cloud of pollution. Concerned air traffic controllers reported the spectacle, radioing headquarters of the sudden appearance of a large blue hole in the sky where moments before a solid brown-grey blanket of smog prevailed. Unfortunately for mankind, when the agency wonks got wind of Drunvalo's toy, the state bureaucracy banished the scientists from performing their beneficial service. Fortunately for me, this was a *lending* library; I devoured Drunvalo's book in the comforts of my own home.

Adrian was big on the Kabbalah. Had this form of metaphysics interested me, I could have learned much, proficient as she was in the ancient secrets of Hermes Trismegistus. Glyphs and symbols I found tedious and distressing; I preferred more direct application to the higher knowledge.

On my next visit to Adrian's oak table, cookies were baking, proffering an atmosphere of home-spun, southern comfort. Her interest focused specifically on my father's training. I related how he emphasized contemplating thoughts carefully before reaching a conclusion; of how he gave little heed to public opinions, pointing out a fatal flaw—most often caused by pride; of how he would alert me when the speaker's ego—the killer of truth—was speaking. That was when my father would warn me quietly: "B.S., Juee, that is total B.S." Quite unintentionally, while learning alongside my father, I began picking up the difference in tone quality of a speaker of truth versus one uttering a falsehood. My father adored the celebrated physician, Dean Edell. But he was revolted by the plethora of misconceived "expert" claims of many others. Pumped up by the proselytizers, claims are often phrased in complicated jargon, "mumbo-jumbo". Such claims sit rotting in mental archives, unchallenged, he would say. Adrian observed that my father was adept at using his sixth principle, *Buddhi*, the intuitive faculties—the vehicle which discriminates between truth and non-truth. Having watched my father's mind penetrating so deeply into natural processes, this made sense. I supposed Adrian was probably right: my father's Buddhic vehicle could explain his advanced abilities in B.S. detection.

Segueing to Dannion Brinkley, she introduced the man who in 1975 died from electrocution for 28 minutes, and then died again on the operating table—but who miraculously recovered to share his experiences of the tunnel and the tutoring angel guides. During a break from a conference on near death experiences (NDEs), an arrogant Ph.D interrupted Dannion's inspired dialogue, demanding to see his qualifications for having formed such an opinion on NDE's. Dannion stood tall, looked the academic straight in his narrow eyes and, with the righteousness that comes from direct knowledge, told the ignorant dissenter: 'I'm Dannion Brinkley, D-O-A!'

At my suggestion, we sat outside under the Tree of Heaven. Picking a nasturtium, I chewed on the stem, enjoying the pungent juice, whetting Adrian's curiosity in the process. She asked me how chlorophyll works. She got the part about how chlorophyll absorbs light energy photochemically. She liked the part about how the electrons are excited to higher energy states, causing a chain of excited electrons holding hands, dancing. She especially loved the part about electrons dancing.

I had been quietly observing the aging murals and informal art in her kitchen, much of it produced long ago by her teenager grandchildren. Her entire house had the appearance of an art gallery, the walls plastered with an assortment of paintings, silk wallhangings and mementos. Two doors always remained closed. Curious, I asked for a peek. One of the two rooms she kept strictly private, demurring. The second door she opened. My first impression was the sanctity of the room, somewhat resembling a museum. Meso-American clay statuettes and Egyptian relics lined two walls. Framed pictures of various divinities hung in neat sections on oak shelving. Crystals and gems were set out neatly on a large antique table. I held up one of the frames, asking the name of the strong face behind the glass.

"That is Master Morya, HPB's guru," Adrian said, walking behind me, picking up another frame about the same size.

"So this is Blavatsky's teacher. Not surprising. He would have to be a strong, masculine force to harness her intensity," I surmised, finding the eyes in the picture fearsome, uncomfortable. "His eyes are quite penetrating, aren't they?"

"Here is a softer face," Adrian said, handing me a dusty frame. I looked easily upon the sensitive face, admiring a graceful man of peace. The eyes exuded a warmth. Such tenderness, I thought.

"Adrian, do you have a cloth, please?" She whisked the picture from me. Wiping off the glass, she put it back in my hands. The clarity now exposed the facial features. The eyes were even softer now. I felt something familiar emerging, a soft glowing seemed to be coming from the face. "Who is this, Adrian? He *feels* familiar but I can't place him."

"That is Koot Hoomi. KH for short. Morya and KH were the Hindu adepts living in Tibet, guiding Blavatsky. Morya was her main dude. It was because of these two that the Theosophical Society came about. Blavatsky was a gifted clairvoyant. Through conveyances across the ethers they tutored her. These are the *Mahatmas*–"great soul" in Sanskrit. Very high adepts, both of them. It's a shame Nell doesn't cotton to this stuff, the invisible world intrigues her, but scares her to death."

Suddenly breathless, in need of oxygen, I went to the kitchen. Retrieving my water glass I wandered outdoors, trembling. Adrian found me sitting on the bench under the Tree of Heaven–calm, but in a state of mild shock. Unfolding in my mind the recent spate of unusual events, I needed the security of the wise Comanche. Never had I needed a wise friend more urgently, at the moment of reckoning: Just moments ago, in Adrian's museum of faces and artifacts, I had made contact at a level of my being that was very much a stranger to myself. In the coming weeks, I would come to know myself much more intimately.

"Adrian, I need to confide in you something that no one else would ever believe."

"I'm listening."

"Back there in your private room I recognized Koot Hoomi from the picture as someone I'd seen before."

"Yes, dear, I was there, remember? Go on, don't be shy."

"Well, when I couldn't breathe, it was because of him! I had a flash, recalling instantly it was Koot Hoomi and Morya who visited me about two months ago–in the flesh, as Jehovah's Witnesses. It's true, I swear it!"

"Well, then honey, congratulations. You have arrived! Most people never do recall these meetings, don't put the pieces together. There's a purpose under heaven, sweetheart. They've come to claim you as their own. *Hallelujah, Jesus*! I am right happy for you, honey. Wipe your tears and give this old girl a big hug."

"That's not all," I said, reviving somewhat; the warmth of her body fat comforting me. Wrapped in the Comanche's arms, my nerves–frayed from the pulsing intensity–soon normalized. Walking back to the kitchen arm-in-arm, I shared with Adrian the mysterious appearance of KH's book the morning just before meeting her for the first time.

"Universal timing is immaculate. Synchronicity. Don't you see how it all fits? You should be pleased with yourself just a wee bit. Masters don't appear in the physical like that very often. It means they're counting on you. You had to be ready before they would come to you in the physical."

"I don't feel very ready. I hardly know much about them."

"Honey, they've known you were ready, otherwise they wouldn't be makin' such a fuss–coming to you as Jehovah's witnesses and leavin' books for you. They've been workin' with you at night for a long time. That's what they do, when we're in our finer bodies at night– without the disruption of daytime business. Sleepin' is when our receptivity is best. That's when they teach us–with our permission of course!–permission from our soul, our higher self, our *I AM*. There is a whole lot to look forward to, young lady. There's stuff I've seen that you don't need to worry yourself about just yet–"

"*Like what*? What don't I need to know just yet? What are you saying, Adrian? Come clean–you're keeping something from me!"

"Hush! Remember silence. My Daddy taught me much about silence. You will *know* what you *need* to know when the time is right."

"I don't think I'm going to like this arrangement, Adrian."

We returned to the subject of Koot Hoomi's book, *Studies of the Human Aura*. I complained that it had been written for the orthodox Christian mind, that after the initial high of recognizing the voice of my teacher–on subsequent readings I had trouble swallowing the Christian pill. Even though the book teaches scientific methods, my free thinking spirit was being rocked about in a dance, juxtaposing science and orthodoxy.

"Well now, Missy. Put this in that big your head of yours: How would you, if you were Koot Hoomi, do it–considering he had to pour that book through the mind of a fundamentalist Christian? He channeled that book through a Christian gentleman by the name of Mark Phophet, the last of the *true* prophets in that entire line of messengers."

"How far back does that line go?"

"In modern times? First it was Blavatsky, then the Roerichs and then Alice Bailey. Then came Godfrey Ray King, followed by Geraldine Innocente. Mark Prophet was the last of the great ones."

"So, that line dried up?"

"Not exactly. After Mark died, his wife lost touch–turned the cult to personality worship: worship of the messenger–rather than the message."

"She lost touch?"

"Too much ego. *Sheesh*, the woman had issues: Had a bad case of the Grandstander malady: Loved power, that one. Yesiree. I've heard her tapes, they taste like cotton candy. Where's the damn beef?

"So, you never saw her in person?"

"Yep. Once was enough. Didn't mean to steer you off track. Let's get back to Koot Hoomi's gift-book to you: he is sending a strong message."

"Message? What message is that?"

"Mark Prophet was the instrument for that book, the last adept in that long line of messengers. It's not every day they find a Blavatsky or a Roerich. They need human vehicles, willin' to be purveyors of the ancient science–reliable bodies down here on earth to let those with ears hear that they actually exist. Missy, you have the ears to hear them. You have the sensitivity to feel them. You have the burning desire to know them. Now, all you need to do is *obey* them!"

"Shiza! You make it sound like a military operation."

"Not so. When you accept the responsibility–and I see you already have–they will definitely let you know when you've wandered off the baseline."

"So, what do I do now, to prepare myself?"

"You listen for their guidance. You just keep on studying your books, keep meditating. You let *them* call the shots. You need to learn patience, Missy. Anyone ever told you that before?"

"I stand humbly corrected."

"Remember this: The Masters need not only us freethinkers, they need *everyone*–all races, creeds, religions–*everyone* is being called. They need light workers, to work with electronic light, heart-centered ones ready to bring in the *Love-Light*, the only *true* way to govern this crazy, mixed-up world we live in, to join our hands to make a rainbow bridge of *Brotherhood* clear across this planet. So, Missy: You read that book again–this time with new eyes, with eyes wide open. Keep your eyes on the Master's goal."

"Half a book, anyway," I corrected her. "Half the book was cut out."

"Someone needed those pages worse than you did, then. Honey, you're digestin' quite a lot in a short spurt. I think you'd best take a run on the beach like you love to do."

I took Adrian's advice. Barefoot, I ran several miles, from Oceano Dunes, north–stopping to treat myself to my favorite flowering *Eucalyptus*. I had the technique down: Forming a suction cup with my lips, working my tongue past the male stamens, down deep into the capsule–I closed my eyes to sample the *myrtaceous* ambrosia–a mixture of semi-sweet honey and mentholated cough drop.

Back on my hill, I wanted to print out Koot Hoomi's picture. Finding his face plastered all over the web, none of them looking like Adrian's Koot Hoomi, I made a quick call to the Comanche. A German artist "Herman something or other" was enough to find *The Portraits of the Mahatmas*. Hermann Schmiechen, I read, was the clairvoyant artist behind the portraits, drawing them in London, July 1884, sketching directly from the Masters' astral presence– with Blavatsky, herself a clairvoyant, correcting occasionally. The article was remarkable and witty. Printing out copies of Morya and KH, I sat back in awe. Oh, my God, I thought to myself, I'm on fire! These guys were my "Jehovah's Witnesses"! How cool is that?

Things began to move fast. With their faces framed, I could meditate with much more efficacy, feeling their souls through the eyes. Obsessing again, I printed more copies, placing them on the table in front of me as I ate dinner, speaking to them as if they were present. I placed them on my piano and at my bedside. Henceforth, with their likenesses surrounding me, their powerful presence was enough to make regular invocations by simply concentrating on them. From then on, weekends were saved for myself: Studying, playing piano, Kriya or gardening, I kept my attention focused on the Masters, staying alert to subtle currents. Listening to the sounds of the wind through the trees, I found myself becoming ultra sensitive to the voices of the nature kingdom. Expecting the Master's *postcards*, I went to bed early: postcards most often came in short phrases and songs in the early morning hours, between 4- to 5 a.m.

I had taken a position at an Arroyo Grande research farm, testing treatments of biopesticides–*Strobilurins* and *Bacillus*–on winegrapes, with field trials in Monterey and Santa Barbara counties. During spring, I walked miles through vineyards, observing signs of disease. At harvest I collected grape samples to measure the old standards: weight, brix, pH and TA. The remaining hours I compiled data for efficacy reports. Working in agriculture, the workday starts very early. My weekends were no different.

Delivered from sleep by a *postcard* at 4:30 a.m. one Saturday, I remained perfectly still, listening to the message. With slow, precision phonetics the word was pronounced: "Por-tee-un-cu-la." That was the entire message. Thanking *Google*, I headed to my Macintosh after a quick morning shower. A straight shot to *Portiuncula or Porziuncola*–the morning's postcard takes me to Italy, where I learn that the *Portiuncula* is: "*a small church located within the Basilica of Santa Maria degli Angeli...situated about 4 kilometres from Assisi.*" I find further that St. Francis restored several ruined churches, among them the *Porziuncola*, his favorite. I was being delivered to the home of St. Francis and his first disciples, to the first home of the Order of Friars Minor.

Too revved up to meditate, I explode into obsessive mode for two solid hours, researching everything about St. Francis– awaiting clues, paying attention to my viscera. Feeling anxious and unreasonably pressed for time, I dressed quickly. Stuffing my mouth with a banana and my pocket full of almonds, I headed the short distance to Adrian's house. Ultimately headed to the Mission San Luis Obispo, I needed some Comanche medicine.

"Adrian, I'm glad you're home. I want to run something by you."

Shutting the door behind me, I relayed my morning news. Barely finishing, she pushed a little blue box in front of me, directing me to open it. Reaching inside, I pulled out a beautiful, 3-dimensional silver star, glowing with iridescent colors.

"This is for you," Adrian said proudly, as though I were being awarded a trophy. "It was sittin' right here on the table this mornin'. From them to me to you. It's a confirmation, dear. They know you worry. Nobody can help you there—it's your nature. But they sure can make things pleasant in sweet little ways, like this here silver star. They want to give you confidence, to keep you keepin' on. Kudos, honey."

What a sweet little silver morning surprise it was. Quite a different surprise I had coming when Adrian flatly refused to answer any of my questions. Instead of information, I got a Comanche lesson in obedience, something about weaning me off any guide other than my teacher, KH. The Comanche stood proud in her rebuff, warning me to be grateful. Unsure of myself, how could I be certain I was interpreting my *postcards* correctly? I begged Adrian to give me her word that she wouldn't desert me. Smiling, she waved me off, giving me no other option but to accept her conditions. 'So, these are the conditions that prevail,' I thought to myself, getting into my truck—remembering the little ditty my father would say when surrendering to the circumstances of life. This was one of those times.

Overwhelmed with the morning's revelations, I missed my turnoff. That "miss" turned into *kismet*—when I pulled right into a slot just vacated, the last parking space of the tiny Mission parking lot. 'Good parking Qi' my old friend used to say to me as we drove around San Francisco, praying for a space. 'You've got to have good parking Qi.' I had been many times to the Catholic Mission, timing my visits to avoid the crowds. Inside the church, I hurried past the altar to the statue of Jesus, just to look into the eyes—so realistic and alive was the face on the statue called *The Sacred Heart*. His pained expression brought tears to my eyes, especially after the morning's message: More than anyone else, St.Francis' love for Jesus was the love of all loves, inspiring many millions to follow in his footsteps.

Saying a blessing, I left Jesus to buy a new rosary at the Mission gift store. For the remainder of the day I grasped at my new rosary, but could find no solace, my mind racing uncontrollably, restless as a little child. Nor could I meditate. I was useless. Driving to *Little Alexandria*, I rushed to the shelf of saints, reading voraciously until I fell into a reverie. Coming out of this contemplative state, I remembered Adrian's words: 'Let them call the shots.' All I could do now was go home to my piano and my cat; nothing seemed to help my wild, uncontrollable condition.

The very next morning I was awakened early with a four letter word: "*FOUR*." Stretching like a cat coming-to, I noticed my new rosary was not on the window ledge where I'd left it the night before. I distinctly remember removing the necklace just before retiring, thinking it too fragile to sleep with me. Touching my neck—Shiza! There it was, the rosary was fastened back onto my neck! Apparently by invisible hands! This was going to be a good Sunday, I could feel it: My invisible helpers were already talking to me and dressing me! *Portiuncula. Four.* I had my homework for the day.

Rather than driving myself mad with thinking, I took a blanket outside for Kriya Yoga. To ameliorate an overactive mind, a dose of indomitable will is key. Bringing my willpower to the forefront, I mentally forced myself into passivity, melting my anxiety into submission. It worked. In meditation on the grass, I focused on my third eye until I was calm. Bringing my word-messages gently into mind, I allowed them to submerge into my being. Lifting my mind from all thoughts whatsoever, I rested in this state of peace. In this state, it became clear: Through what I would call a gentle, yet fiery flash—I indeed received confirmation: I saw myself pictured as the fourth friar of St.Francis' original band of monks!

Like a happy child, I went skipping across the lawn, into my office. Onwards to my Macintosh. I had already bookmarked

Fioretti di San Francesco–Little Flowers of St.Francis, an anthology
of intimate stories told by St.Francis' friars themselves. Reading of
Frate Masseo's description of Saint Francis preaching to the birds
was a glorious beginning. When I came to the fourth friar, "Frate
Egido," or "Giles," I was reading about myself nearly 800 years ago.
As Giles, it says I was raised to the third heaven and experienced
ecstasies. I was the monk who had a vision of Christ at Cetona. It
even said about Giles, that he–or that *I* was considered the most
perfect example of the primitive Franciscan. St. Francis called me
his "Knight of the round table." Reading on, I found that as Giles,
my writings were noted for their humor, deep understanding of
human nature and optimism. I couldn't help but see the similarity.
The difference was in the words we used back then. The *Fioretti* had
many examples:

*Brother Giles was asked about humility: "It seems to me that holy
humility is like the thunderbolt; for, even as the thunderbolt striketh a
terrible blow, crushing, breaking, and burning that whereon it lights,
yet can we never find the thunderbolt itself, so does humility strike and
disperse, burn up and consume every evil and vice and sin, and yet
itself can nowhere be seen."*

*A friar once said to Brother Giles: "Father, it seems to me that we have
not yet learned to know our true good." And Brother Giles replied:
"My brother, it is certain that every one practices the art which he had
learned, for no man can do good work unless he has first learned. I
would have thee to know then, my brother, that the most noble art in
the world is that of well-doing; and who can know it except he first
learn it?"*

*Then Brother Giles said to a certain friar: "Father, I would fain know
what is contemplation?" And the friar answered: "Father, truly I know
not." Then Brother Giles said: "To me it seems that contemplation is a
divine fire, a sweet devotion infused by the Holy Ghost, a rapture and
suspension of the mind inebriated by the unspeakable savour of divine
sweetness, and a sweet and tranquil enjoyment of the soul which is rapt
and suspended in loving admiration of the glories of heaven, and an*

inward and burning consciousness of that celestial and unspeakable glory."

As soon as time allowed, I met up with Adrian in Pismo–I couldn't wait to share the revelation. Adrian was adamant as flint about weaning me off her guidance and onto KH. I respected her wisdom but I still wanted to hear her thoughts.

"Yep," she agreed, "you sound just like Giles all right. Damn, you haven't changed much" she giggled as we sat in the sun on Nell's balcony, reading choice quotes from the *Fioretti*. They were in full agreement with the historians, who record Giles as having a sardonic wit, an acidulous and testy tongue. The books record him as being shrewd and racy. I rested my case. I didn't need the Comanche this time.

For the first time in my life, I felt free to share with these good friends my childhood visitation, about the chanting monks who droned to me in my bedroom:

"God child, God child, God child, God child, God child..."

"To develop the full might of this Science, the discords of corporeal sense must yield to the harmony of spiritual sense, even as the science of music corrects false tones and gives sweet concord to sound.

"The physical healing of Christian Science results now, as in Jesus' time, from the operation of divine Principle, before which sin and disease lose their reality in human consciousness and disappear as naturally and as necessarily as darkness gives place to light and sin to reformation. Now, as then, these mighty works are not supernatural, but supremely natural."

For verily I say unto you, That whosoever shall say unto this mountain,

Be thou removed, and be thou cast into the sea; and shall not doubt in his heart, but shall believe that those things which he saith shall come to pass; he shall have whatsoever he saith.

Therefore I say unto you, What things soever ye desire, when ye pray, believe that ye receive them, and ye shall have them.

Your Father knoweth what things ye have need of before ye ask Him-Jesus Christ"

Here, on Adrian's table lay my next lesson. Excusing herself, Adrian left me to ponder the thoughts of Mary Baker Eddy, the originator of Science of the Mind.

"The only word I object to is the use of 'sin.' I can accept it out of the mouth of an early Franciscan monk, but here, the word 'sin' bothers me."

"Oh, don't get your knickers knotted! Why get stuck on the language? Just feel the essence of what she's saying."

I had to appreciate Adrian's direct manner. There was no room for any vagueness in her life; she would swat it away like a fly. My father was direct and that virtue was what drew me close to Sri Yukteswar, Yogananda's guru. Yogananda said of his teacher: "Sri Yukteswar's intuition was penetrating: heedless of remarks, he often replied to one's unexpressed thoughts....I daresay he would have been the most sought-after guru in India had his speech not been so candid."

"Adrian, you remind me of my first guru, Sri Yukteswar. He left no room in his ashram for B.S., so direct was he–like you. Only the devoted and diligent chelas could handle his strict policies and his critiques. Look at what perfection he sculpted–his methods gave us Yogananda, for one example! It's Sri Yukteswar's photo I keep in my wallet. He was actually my first Indian guru. Yogananda's respect for him made him my own."

"Whatever works well for your mind works for your growth. Now, if you don't mind–back to the table: What did you think of Mary Baker Eddy's writings. Did they resonate with you at all?"

"Resonate, yes–that's a good word to use, I did feel them. I couldn't help thinking of Pantanjali's eight limbs. Her ideas are similar to Kriya Yoga–especially where she talks about yielding to the harmony of spiritual sense, "even as the science of music corrects false tones and gives sweet concord to sound," I emphasized, reading from the document. "Her thoughts read like a description of the sympathetic vibrations of physics–but in a slightly different context."

"Goody." Adrian chirped. Leaving her personal past out, Adrian had not shared with me what her daughter shared years later: Adrian had been an avid Christian Scientist when her children were young. "I just wanted you to taste the similarities in these great minds. I also wanted you to know a wee bit of what my Mama taught me when I was growin' up in Texas."

"So you had a double dose of the mind sciences growing up–half Kabbalah and half Christian Science. Not bad for a country Texan."

"Not bad for a half-breed, eh?"

Chapter 33 Apache Medicine

Whence does one derive strength and wisdom? In union with the Great Spirit, recognizing cause and motive, we build an immediate consequence. We evoke Those who earlier did set out on the great path of personal realization and responsibility. And our appeals, through thousands of raised hands, reach Them.

El Morya

"**W**ell, hello *Golden Girl*!!" The charge boomed mega-coulombs of fiery force directly at me. I stood back, well behind my aunt–shying away like a frightened filly. Never in recent memory had anyone carried a force strong enough to intimidate me so. The blast was so unexpected, coming from the tiny frame and exiting through the ruby-painted lips–on top of which was mounted a huge mane of bright auburn hair. This was certainly going to be an interesting visit, I thought, wondering what my aunt–who lived next door to the 85-year-old–had gotten me into. "Katie," had just months before relocated to San Diego from Texas, and was quickly becoming known as one possessing special powers. I had just come from Sedona, AZ, enjoying my first Native American Pow-Wow–now spending a few weeks visiting my parents. Within the hour, it became clear that Katie and I would need to visit together again, privately.

Within the week I returned. Barely past the doorway threshold, I cornered her straightaway: "Katie, what made you boom out *Golden Girl* at our first meeting?"

"Well sweetheart, you just about *blinded* me, that's why! Your aura is a big, bright sight. Big as day."

"So my aura's gold?"

"Yesiree, honey, big as a rainbow." Not one to be tied down, Katie was about to break off onto another track when I stopped her cold.

"Katie, please! Come back to the *Golden Girl*. Please describe exactly what you see in my aura."

"Well honey, there's a saint overtop you. You already *know* that! Why ask me?"

"No, I don't *know* that. I *am* working with a teacher, yes, that's true. What does my *saint* look like?"

"Slender...prime of life...long hair...beard. Handsome too!"

"Katie, would you mind waiting just one moment, please? I have a picture I want to show you." I ran out the door to my truck, not bothering to wait for a reply. Out of breath, I handed Katie a laminated travel version of Hermann Schmiechen's Koot Hoomi. She studied the face of Master KH.

"Yesiree, that's him! Damn honey, *he is fine*! Looks to me like he'd want to *do it real slow.*" Embarrassed by her sultry slithering, I sat motionless while Katie purred–unabashed–at the attractive face, showing no signs of modesty. I had never heard anyone speak of the Masters in a sexual context. Her raciness threw me into a zone of quiet, wondering what to expect next from the lascivious lips of the octogenarian.

"Katie, was this saint with me the first time you met me," I inquired of the smitten woman, bringing her back to the present. She had no intention of removing herself from her semi-ecstatic state. It made me squirm to watch her unload her animal musk so irreverently.

"He never leaves you! He's with you all the time!" Katie's voice boomed again. Looking over my aura, I saw her smile–and then wink–at something in the air above me. This woman was a veteran mystic, her psychic abilities impressive. "You are protected!"

"But my saint protects others as well, yes?" I already knew the answer.

"Oh yes, they are *very* busy. Protect thousands. They can spark up their heavenly body in as many places as they wish–all at once–whenever they want," she said. "Let's have some fresh melon. Come on, follow me. I held on to one of these...survived the white stuff, you know, the whatchamacallit..."

"Mildew?"

"Yes, that's it. Plus, I got me some squirrels that come for dinner. They can sure make a mess of things. But I don't quarrel, there's plenty for everyone." Katie managed a vegetable garden in her back yard, with fresh cucurbits, beans, corn and tomatoes. Being a gardener, I was impressed. Again. I could not get past her vigor, her tempo. She had a striking sense of well being–peppy and vivacious. She mentioned a son who comes to help sometimes. She was still driving herself to the market.

"My cousin tells me you worked for the Texas police," I inquired, slurping juice from the succulent cantaloupe. I had heard colorful stories about Katie's clairvoyance.

"Long time ago I did. You see, ever since I was a child, I had this ability to see things that other people couldn't see. I call it my *long-vision*. Made my Momma afraid of me. Preacher told everyone at church I was a witch. Mostly people just gossiped and stayed clear away from me."

" And your father?"

"Gone! My Mamma told me he died, but I knew it wasn't true. We'll get to that part later. Anyway, the police used my *long-vision* to search for missing children. It really got to me after a while. They begged me to stay but I was gettin' sick from what I saw–children dead in rivers, down ravines, eaten away by wild animals...some other ways I won't ever talk about again."

"So, this *long-vision*–did you have a special method you used?"

"Well, it helped if I could touch something they wore, to hold it and smell it. Police said my face got all funny. Sheriff put me in his office, showed me pictures if he had some. Gave me the kid's clothes and things, you know–anything like that. He'd leave me alone in there. That's about it."

"How long did it take to see the missing children?"

"Sometimes 2 minutes! Sometimes days."

"And you always found the children?"

"Always. That's why I couldn't do it anymore. Awful, made me sick."

"And do you have that ability still?"

"Sweetheart, you never lose it. Now I just soar. Do you like to soar?"

"What? Uh...well, actually, yes. I do like to soar," I said, surprised. Suddenly in perfect tune with the tenured mystic, I sensed a kinship, a parity. "I've practiced a type of Hindu Yoga for many years now. When I meditate–at a certain point I always fly into space. I move through the galaxy, the stars. I guess I'd have to say I soar on a daily basis."

"Did you hear that? *"Frequent flyer!"* Your saint just called you a *frequent flyer!* Welcome aboard, honey!"

Like Adrian, Katie was a rare breed, another 'half-breed' whose Apache father left the family when she was born, her Irish mother claiming he was dead–denying young Katie her Native American Indian heritage. She caught up to her father only much later in life. Watching her speak, the high cheek bones gave her away, pronouncing the unmistakable *Apache* origins, especially when she smiled–and Katie was always smiling.

"Ever since I was little I knew I was Indian–found out everything I could about my breed. Had some Indian friends, too. At 15, I went lookin' for my blood line. By then, I knew about my saint.

Got plenty of help from my saint, *BIG* help!

"Who is your saint, Katie? What's his name?"

"Hell, I don't know and don't care! Doesn't matter. I know he's with me and that's enough for me."

"Katie, I keep a collection of saints' faces with me wherever I go. I want to know which one is yours," I insisted, running to my truck again, returning to her side. I pulled out images one-by-one for her to see.

"That's him! That's my saint," Katie squealed in delight, hugging the image of St.Germain. This is a Master well known for his gifts to humanity, generously allotting a part of his *causal* body–amassed over many lifetimes–to the earth, thereby infusing the planet with a great endowment of the high-frequency violet flame. The violet flame is known for it efficacious atomic cleansing capabilities, it's ability to erase karmic scars in man as well as the natural environment. Katie didn't seem to be too interested in the science. She had personal meetings to recount, which are so much more meaningful. She told me how St.Germain had saved her life on two different occasions–both times her feverish condition had reached dangerous proportions. Each time the saint healed her miraculously, leaving for Katie signs confirming that his presence was real. I gifted Katie with St.Germain's picture. Quiet repose not being her specialty, Katie wanted to finish her Apache saga.

"So, anyway, my saint helped me find my tribe–he led me to the Apaches livin' in New Mexico. Soon as I could, I made my way over to those parts. Walked right in, demanded to speak with the chief medicine man. They said no, said I wasn't no Apache. But they didn't know what they had comin'. I let 'em have it! I wasn't taking 'no' for an answer. I camped out, right there. Refused to go away till I had my meetin' with the big chief. I let 'em know I meant business."

Being born with Apache warrior-blood paid off–that and righteous persistence. Picturing the obdurate redhead camping outside the Apache chief's doorstep was not difficult. She won her victory: Katie was brought into the tribe *ex-officio*, due to her *signs*: Examining her carefully, the tribal elders found that Katie exhibited all the signs of an Apache medicine woman, promptly anointing her as protégé to the head medicine chief. So began her stay on the reservation, learning the Apache Way. In time she was taught the herbal mixtures for what she called the '*Big Smoke*'–which, I was surprised to learn–included small amounts of marijuana. The *Big Smoke,* she said, was a very special ceremony, when the elders made sacred invocations to *Great Spirit.* Katie would not describe any more, saying she was already out of line with Apache probity for telling me this much. Who could blame her for going over the baseline? Revivifying her Apache Odyssey, her wrinkled face beamed like the noonday sun. Recalling the days of her bloodline reckoning, Katie began making invocations right there in her living room, uttering blessings–*fortissimo*–thanking *Great Spirit* for giving her entrance into the Apache Way, *medicine* that had been long overdue.

"That's an amazing story, absolutely amazing".

I made one final trip to Katie's before returning up north to Hummingbird Hill. Knowing I wouldn't be back any time soon, I requested her clairvoyant services. "Katie," I began sheepishly, "would you do me a huge favor? I need your *long vision* to help me to confirm something."

I had shared with the auburn Apache the visitation I received years back of the white *Swan-Dove,* coming apparently to steer me away from the dark abyss of my own making: my obsession with the mystery man. I relayed to her the recent spate of *postcards,* all of which linked me in two past lives with this man: The *postcards* lead directly to Spain and then to Scotland–revealing past lives when we had been married, not once–but twice–in successive lifetimes! No wonder there was such a strong connection. Although the *postcards* detailed for me those incarnations, I refrained from sharing them with Katie. I was testing her medicine.

"Do you have anything he touched?" she asked.

"Not physically, no" but I have something that touched *him*." I had come prepared for the mystic: From the truck I returned with a downloaded photograph of the mystery man and a letter. The letter was the sole business correspondence between us, an email I had sent him. Having taken exquisite care in the wording, I made certain he would not miss the subtle, underlying meaning. Without literally saying so, I amazed even myself at the soulful, "pulling" effect of my tender wording, knowing full well the arrow was aimed perfectly, certain to hit the target–his heart. In abscentia, I could feel him as he began to read the letter: It was late afternoon. I felt his heart pounding as he read. When he finished reading the letter, his heart was so heavy he lost complete feeling in his legs. From afar I knew for certain he had been seized by the carefully-crafted syntax and the subtle innuendos. At that crowning moment, I witnessed the truth of the old saying: *The pen is mightier than the sword.* I felt him as he slumped in his chair, motionless. His pain deep, he sat for some time, powerless to move.

"Sounds like you don't need me, sweetheart, you're a seer, all right." Katie seemed pleased with my account, pleased to see me developing mystically–her words striking me as a rerun of the hours under Adrian's tutelage. "I knew you the first time I saw you. You have everything you need already. You don't need me."

"Please Katie, I lack confidence. This stuff takes time. I want to be *absolutely* certain. Confirmation from someone of your capabilities means a great deal to me."

"All right, I'll sleep on it tonight, that's when I do my best work these days."

"Katie, one more thing–I want to give you one clue: Our past life together in Spain took place in the 1400s."

Chapter 34   *The Rain in Spain*

*Of the five senses beholding to man, if one springeth a leak, then
from that single hole runneth out all his intelligence, even like water
running out from a perforated leathern vessel.*

Mahabharata, Vidur Niti. The Wisdom of Vidura

Topping off the tank, our bodies also needed fuel. We entered
through the door under the sign reading "Asian Noodle Cafe."
Passing statues of the Laughing Buddha, we took a table for two
in the back of the tiny establishment, near the kitchen. Unable to
determine the nationality from the art designs, Naomi and I played
at guessing until the waitress came to take our order.

"We are from Vietnam," came the answer in a soft whisper,
reminding me of the pleasing characteristics of the Asian culture,
their beautiful voices and their modesty. I remembered the several
crushes I had on Asian men, which had come to nothing more
than that.

"I'll have a Thai ice tea and the Mongolian tofu lunch special
please," I told the pretty lady.

"I'll have the same, but add a serving of your egg rolls, please,"
Naomi smiled, making an exaggerated gesture of gratitude,
thanking the strong whiff coming from the kitchen, sending Asian
spices floating across our table.

A friend of many years, Naomi had invited me for a weekend
road trip. Now midway to our destination we were anticipating a
relaxing stay at Shasta Mountain. I had heard about the bookstores
from Adrian; it was a perfect time to gather literary resources.

"So," Naomi asked, "you had a good visit with your parents?"

"Always. I must have done something right to have earned such wonderful parents. They never put any pressure on me to be anything other than what I wanted to be. Of course, Dad was very strict with all the important things, but after that it was up to us."

"I suppose I could say the same thing about mine, but during their divorce everything sort of went haywire. We all made it back in time to enjoy the adult years. So, you were telling me about your Irish-Apache friend–"

"Where did I leave off? Oh, yes, I remember. Katie took my fantasy-man's picture and the letter with her that night and performed what she called simply 'Apache Medicine'–an invocation to *Great Spirit,* I believe. I asked about her system but she was mum on the subject. Just like my other Indian friend, Adrian, both of them warned me not to allow anyone, including them, to interfere with KH's teaching–insisting that I no longer require any earthbound teacher, that I should pay attention *only* to the messages coming directly from KH."

"That's sage advice. I was told to stay away from psychics. I think my friend's words were: 'Avoid them like poison.' So, Katie wouldn't confirm anything?"

"Only out of mercy. She would only say that I was correct. I pushed her harder and she repeated herself, saying that what I already knew was correct. She warned me not to involve anyone else. Almost sounded like an order."

"So, that must mean she was in contact with KH?"

"I asked her that question directly. She looked at me like 'DUH'! I got a lesson in Apache probity, a spanking really, as if I should be grateful for the Apache medicine, but in silence. The lesson was that I wasn't supposed to verbally thank an Apache for their medicine– they find it offensive. This is the *Apache Way,* that the 'Great Spirit' knows all things, so don't mangle the blessing with words. Words become superfluous, meaningless. In my case, anyway, they created a mess."

"So, have you told anyone about...Spain?"

"Only you. I am not sure I'm ready to share that. How do you tell someone that you were part of the Inquisition? Someday, I will share that with my mystery man. I think he needs to know about our past life as Ferdinand and Isabella. Shiza! What will he do with that information? As far as I know, he has no background in spiritual science—he might flip out!"

"I think it's your duty to tell him. He can do with it what he likes."

"I know it has helped me to understand many things about myself. KH told me the karma I accrued 600 years ago is the last vestiges I have to work out—that this is my last go-round here. I get to escape this ghastly place, I've earned my freedom this lifetime. I'll be ascending after this, thank God!"

"Roger that. Knowing past lives could be of real value, finding the real causes of our obsessions. Probably knocks off years of therapy."

"You're funny. Did I tell you about the *postcard* words and songs in my ear, leading me up to the *Inquisition* revelation?"

"Songs? What songs?"

"'*Hello Muddah, hello Faddah, here I am at Camp Granada*' was one of them."

"Omigod, that is hilarious."

"Another time it was: '*The rain in Spain lays mainly on the plain.*'"

"Sounds like you're having fun with your Master."

"He's very funny, a dry sense of humor. I wouldn't be listening to someone shaming me in judgement. One time he gave me the word 'Sangria.' Do you know what that means in Spanish?"

"Spanish blood! Whoa, KH is pretty direct, isn't he? Tell me, Jules, do you feel regret now that you know? I'm not sure what I would do with that information, personally."

"I went through the shame and blame until I was blue in the face. I tried to deny it, reading the various accounts–choosing to agree with the ones recording me as a passive wife–subject to my husband's wishes, that *he* was the one in charge of it. Another opinion says the opposite. All I know is that I was *very* Catholic. *Devout* and thought I was doing the right thing. To answer your question, yes! Of course I regret my actions. How could anyone subject thousands of people to choose between exile, conversion to Catholicism or death? I cried a river for those Jews and Islamic people–the wretchedness and suffering of another Diaspora. Look at me now: I cry at the sight of a dead squirrel in the road. I can't bear to watch violent movies. I don't even own a TV. I can't listen to the news. I'm super, super sensitive in this incarnation. My Master mentioned that. No, actually that was Master Morya who told me that."

"How many teachers speak with you? KH and Morya...who else."

"Well, I have several who have spoken to me on occasion. Yogananda and his guru, Sri Yukteswar, Krishna, Saint Germain and Sanat Kumara."

"You've been busy!"

"It's not quite like that. They speak when I go to *them*, when I invoke *them*. With one exception: I'm not sure which initiation it is, because different books say different things–but they all agree that when Santa Kumara approaches you, it indicates a certain level of attainment and signifies a specific initiation. I was outside my parent's house when he came–in voice only–and said: 'I am the voice of many waters.' I had to research that one, I had no idea who it was that approached me."

"He's in the Bible. Sanat Kumara is known as 'The Voice of Many Waters' and 'The Ancient of Days.' In the Hindu pantheon he is known as Karttikeya. You know what? Hearing about your initiations is making me feel I'm falling behind."

"We'd better get back on the road, Naomi."

"You're right. I want to get to Shasta before the sun sets."

Chapter 35 Tracking the Maha Chohan

O Bharata, the soul is spoken of as a river; religious merit constitutes its sacred baths; truth, its water; self-control, its banks; kindness, its waves. He that is righteous purifieth himself by a bath therein, for the soul is sacred, and the absence of desire is the highest merit.

Mahabharata, Vidur Niti, The Wisdom of Vidura

At the southern reaches of the Cascade Range stands magnificent Mount Shasta at 14,179 feet, well known as a magnetic vortex. On a mission to pick up rare and out of print books, Adrian had guaranteed we would be, at the very least, inspired by the beautiful white mountains in Siskiyou County, California. Many seekers claim to have harnessed great energy fields here; some say they were changed forever. I was not too interested in the energies. I had much to process with the kaleidoscope of "postcards" from my Master Koot Hoomi. My mind was set on spending hours browsing through as many bookstores as I could in the two days at our disposal.

From the moment we arrived, I felt almost overwhelmed by the admixture of numerous and different energies presenting themselves. After browsing a few of the NewAge establishments, I felt inebriated by the information overload of the too-familiar assortment of angel artwork, bright colored mandalas, incense, gems, and Buddhas. The mystical emporium of the town's atmosphere was not what I was after—each new shop a repetition of the one I had just left. I was hungry for something original, authentic—something deeper than the deity menageries flooding the marketplace. Naomi agreed.

We stopped for a cool ice tea and sat on a bench in the shade of an old Birch tree, a short way from the crowds. That is when I heard it—a low buzzing tone on the F key, some octaves below middle C. Droning in my ear was a humming sound, much like the mantric 'AUM,' an electrical current producing tangible, vibratory conductivity. Looking up at the utility wires, I thought I would find the source–sounding not unlike the 'hum-buzz' of electrical cables. My friend could not hear anything other than the blackbirds just above us, perched in a neat row on the wires. As I focused on the sound, the drone seemed to get louder, yet not overly loud, but consistent. I rose to begin my hunt, in pursuit of the strange low frequencies now making their presence known by a slight compression on my heart–causing me to inhale deeply to expand my lung cavity. Thinking of water witching, I put out my hand, trying to feel the path of the current–retracing my steps back when the humming diminished or lessened in intensity. After a time, I sat back down with Naomi to finish my tea, requesting pure silence. Impatient, I began to wonder if the hum was just my imagination. We gathered our belongings in silence and crossed the street.

It was Naomi who chose to enter the unremarkable shop. I followed her quick steps into a small building with nothing in the storefront windows other than some posters and miniature Buddhas. Once inside, the hum returned. Delighted, I turned to smile a secret "thank you" at Naomi, but she had spied something of interest and was already meandering down an isle to see some treasure in the moment of some inspiration. Innocence like Naomi's works wonders: Whereas pushing boundaries in a state of impetuosity–my natural inclination–will get the pilgrim only half way there–humble patience escorts the pilgrim effortlessly to the goal.

A simply framed picture drew me. Hanging alone on the back wall, I knew I had seen those eyes before. Somewhere, I had received the *medicine* from those very eyes–so deep, so serious, yet full of compassion at the same time. I immediately inquired of the noble face wrapped in the white turban.

"You are referring to the '*Maha Chohan*,' the clerk mumbled distractedly, returning to his book.

"Do you have any books on the Maha Chohan, I inquired, in a tone emphasizing I wanted the information *yesterday*.

"Over there on the top row," he waved, pointing to nowhere in particular, apparently unwilling to take his customer seriously, his eyes riveted on his book. I laughed to myself, thinking back to my Indian maidens, Adrian and Katie–both of whom had refused to oblige my incessant questioning, instructing me to discern wisdom silently, independently, patiently. I checked on Naomi, who was quite content–amusing herself with a series of Tibetan singing bowls. With some difficulty I found one book by the turbaned Master and, pulling from the row three more books, I returned to the counter, beginning at once to mine the clerk's brain for knowledge on the noble face.

"Excuse me, but may I ask you a few questions, please?"

"Certainly," came the response. He pulled himself away from a yellow book he was devouring, setting it aside on the counter.

"Can you tell me something about the Maha Chohan? I have not heard of him."

"His name in Sanskrit means *Great Lord*. He is overlord of the Hierarchy of Masters of Wisdom, overseeing all activities of the Chohans of the seven rays, dispenser of earth's energies. He's responsible for the progress of this civilization at large...quite an imposing figurehead. It is the Maha Chohan who oversees the nature kingdom, as well."

"Those are quite the credentials–amazing. What a workload! He would have to be brilliant to handle all that responsibility."

"I should say so. His past embodiments indeed bear that out. He was embodied as Orpheus, Homer as well as Virgil. Going back to Vedic times, he was Vidura, the sage of wisdom and statecraft, councillor to King Dhritarashtra of the *Mahabharata*–the Hindu epic."

The *Illiad* and *Odyssey* I had read. I had a CD of Gluck's opera *Orfeo ed Euridice*. I knew Dante adored Virgil, but I had not read the *Aeneid*. I had admired the rustic poems of Virgil's *Ecologues*, intrigued by his kinship with agricultural life in the *Georgics*. Little else registered. "Do you have any books on Orpheus?" I had elicited the clerk's attention. We shared similar interests.

"Well, it so happens I am reading *Orpheus*. Would you be interested in a publication by Édouard Schuré?"

"Whatever you recommend. Yes, please. It must be good, I noticed you were devouring the book. One more thing: Do you sell prints of the Maha Chohan's picture?"

"I believe we may have a few left. One moment please."

Striking the mine for all its worth, I felt inordinately rich. I had struck gold, or rather–Naomi had: It was her footsteps that led us into the humble little establishment. I thought to myself, smiling broadly, Naomi must have good "book Qi."

"Oh, and Koot Hoomi?" You must have his books," I remembered as the clerk returned with a print.

"Yes, of course. You are aware that the Maha Chohan was Koot Hoomi's superior during the establishment of the Theosophical Society."

"No, I was not. I must be on the right path," I said, restraining myself from a sudden urge to launch into my *postcards* from the Master, reminding myself the clerk must be barraged with such accounts, especially here in the heart of the mystical mountain.

"Have you read *The Mahatma Letters,* actual correspondence from KH during those early formative years of the TS? It's really a must read if you're interested in him on a personal level. The original letters are on display in the British Museum."

"Absolutely! *The Mahatma Letters* was on my list! Oh, thank you for your help, I almost forgot."

"That would be over here," he said, curling around a narrow isle crowded with literary gems. I followed him like a puppy, close on his heels.

"What do we have here?" I asked, pointing to a stack of Krishnamurti paperbacks. "Is Krishnamurti big in Shasta?"

"Not currently. He was an early pioneer of the higher, eastern wisdom. Quite an independent thinker–a major icon for the TS's establishment until he disbanded himself completely from the TS and moved to Ojai. This was some years after Blavatsky's passing. It's a long story, but a very interesting one."

"So, what was Krishnamurti's connection to Koot Hoomi?"

"KH had ascended sometime in the late 1800s, no one knows exactly when...but we do know, from Leadbeater's writings, that both KH and Maitreya guided the young Krishnamurti."

Floating on a literary high, I couldn't wait to tell my Father about the Krishnamurti-KH connection, wondering what his response would be. Here I was, after all these years, imbibing the delicious flavor of enhanced relationship. In just one afternoon–in a hole-in-the-wall bookstore in Shasta–the discovery that my father and I shared an amazing guru connection unfolded: *His guru*, Krishnamurti, had been taught by *my guru*, KH! I was getting richer by the minute.

Chapter 36 The Return of the Dove

Sacrifice, study, charity, asceticism, truth, forgiveness, mercy, and contentment constitute the eight different paths of righteousness. The first four of these may be practised from motives of pride, but the last four can exist only in those that are truly noble.

Mahabharata, Vidur Niti. The Wisdom of Vidura

Walking briskly up the mountain trail, moving away from Naomi–I found myself in desperate need of perfect solitude. The wilderness of the Cascades draws many visitors. My cup had runneth over with enough strangers' faces to last for a month or two. My dear friend very obligingly allowed me my sudden obsession, allowing me to wander off in search of the nearest spot I could find resembling a hermetically-sealed space of earth. Responding to signals, I needed to listen to the intense inspiration coming from inside me. Hiking up the mountain trail, well ahead of Naomi–I seated myself on pine needles, out of view from passing hikers.

It was a good call–I soon received a most extraordinary bird visitor. In my peripheral vision a charcoal black bird landed no more than five feet away. Welcoming all bird-friends, I turned to see which avian had joined me. To my surprise and pleasure, I beheld a black-toned Starling who became, a moment later, a magnificently multicolored creature–nearly startling me–so vivid did his markings glow. Intuiting that I was in the presence of something out of the mist, and knowing the Starling's predilection for the city, I mused on what the beautiful flyer was doing here in the mountains. Pondering the ornithological incongruency, the bird halted my faulty track–looking at me directly. In silence he communicated he was no ordinary Starling, reproaching me gently for my foolishness–communicating that I already *knew he was Spirit*. When next moment his many hued feathers began changing colors, I beheld the Starling's human eyes– recognizing their somber expression from a former visit–

"O sweet friend, my Swan-Dove, you have come again," I sang to my old friend.

But there was no bowing of his head this time. I was past the punishing pain at the time of the Swan-Dove's visit. The Starling's countenance, here on the magnetic vortex of Shasta, was one of friendship–as if he were approaching a comrade, as if he were asking for my cooperation. I sensed he had serious business to conduct with me this day.

Red! Pink! Blue! Green! Yellow! Orange! Such sudden flashing from his feathers–the bright colors highlighted themselves in a series of changes, merging into brilliant tones, dazzling me in amazement. When the avian light show paused, the Starling's eyes contained not an ounce of showmanship, but rather, a face of some European noblesse, and I understood: This was *not* a light-show for amusement, these were critical teachings for my instruction. Resorting to girlish excitement a moment before, I had nervously misread the phenomenon, so mesmerized was I by the extraordinary array of light. From the bird's eyes I came to understand that I was being trained to focus on the light rays specifically, the solar rays used by the ascended Masters. My Starling friend did not stay long. Instructing me in the operation of laser light rays, he departed.

Immediately positioning myself for meditation, I closed my eyes, shutting out everything but the extraordinary Starling. Reaching the soundless silence, merging into a calm state of receptivity–nothing could have prepared me for the shock: In my third eye shone the solemn face of the Maha Chohan, the *Maha Sahib* of the heavenly hierarchy who oversees not only civilization, but the nature kingdom! I should have put it together before. Visual artists never forget facial features, but I was not among those so gifted, remembering voices, colors and patterns. Stunned, I sat inhaling the resins of the pines needles, relishing the most astonishing revelation: Yes! The eyes of both my avian visitors–the Swan-Dove *and* the Starling–are those of the Maha Chohan!

These eyes were described by KH as the 'implacable Chohan,' the top chief in command over KH and Morya in their Herculean efforts to establish the Theosophical Society. Known for his stern appearance and far-reaching wisdom, his superior orders are obeyed as the last word. Known also as a ruby ray Master, the Maha Chohan's visit meant that I was to be trained in the use of the ruby laser light, known for its efficacy in projection and penetration.

Training in the ruby ray can assist the hierarchy in the cleansing and removal of astral debris—the astral plane being a literal cesspool of negative thought forms created by human minds; thoughts which have contaminated the lower octaves in which we live. Buddha himself said it simply:

"We are what we think. All that we are arises with our thoughts. With our thoughts, we create the world."

Chapter 37 The Pistachio Nut Fairy

One should restrain one's lust and stomach by patience;
one's hands and feet by one's eyes; one's eyes and ears by one's mind;
and one's mind and words by one's acts.

Mahabharata, Vidur Niti, The Wisdom of Vidura

"Naomi, I need your opinion on something that's been dogging me." Drying ourselves with huge spa towels after an evening under the stars, my friend and I had spent the hours hopping back and forth from the outdoor sauna to the hot tub. The air was crisp, the night sky clear, our skin shriveled, prune-like.

"Shoot."

"In the *Mahatma Letters* and in what he conveyed through Blavatsky in *The Secret Doctrine*, KH speaks as a pure Buddhist, consistently illustrating cosmic law as the one universal source of life—even castigating the men of the cloth for their ignorant notion of a personal God. What's bewildering me is that, in *The Studies of the Human Aura*, KH speaks of 'Children of the one God' or that 'Christ consciousness is the mediator between God and man'—referring to God in the sense of a personal being—utterly un-Buddhistic statements. It seems to me there's a contradiction about the nature of God in his works. Help me out here."

"That's not too difficult when you consider the amanuensis taking the *Aura* dictation was a fundamentalist Christian! Pardon the levity here but—don't you see that it would be a *fundamental* mistake on KH's part if he had tried to reach into a fundamentalist's mind using a Buddhist teaching?

"Yes. Keep going."

"Belief systems run deep, especially so for Christian evangelist-types. They'd be likely to kill the Buddhist message! Force-fed orthodoxy so long, the mental stylus of Christianity has dug deep into their psyche. Years of engraving dogma deep into a platinum LP, the recording lives on. How could someone consuming an orthodox diet be expected to suddenly find to their liking a concept suggesting they've been fooled their whole life?

"KH does admonish the sacerdotal caste, saying they're the cause of all wars."

"So, how does KH get past the dogma barrier? He speaks in a language more suitable." Naomi was well read, a scholar who evoked understanding with her precise simplicity. Unlike me, she excelled in math. "How would you teach Euclid's ideas to a child?"

"I wouldn't know where to begin on the subject of Euclid. I suppose I might try feeding them sugar-coated candy, to draw them in."

"Slowly, that's how. You teach by reflecting one facet of the diamond mind at a time. You begin with the heart, otherwise you can't speak to the soul. It's at the soul level that you truly teach–that's what lures the lamb from the safety of the fold. KH knows what burns in a Christian's heart–Christ! There's no language barrier there."

"I've had a crush on Jesus ever since I was a child," I sang, energized by my friend's brilliance. "Christ burns in my heart too, and I'm no orthodox anything!" Memories of my youth interpenetrated the nighttime exchange, the clear song of my life emerging. My *Keynote*, my *Ode* transposed itself melodically as images began to flash across the screen of life. I stood by, as if at a distance–the song of my *Presence* emerging. Notwithstanding the treasures–the new psychologies and esoteric philosophies–I had not changed one bit since childhood. Self-actualized from following only the true north of my soul's will, I knew that I never would.

"Of course, mine too and I'm a Jew," Naomi began again, catching me–bringing me back from the slipstream. "Jesus is among the greatest teacher of all avatars. His teachings ended up mangled by a sleight-of-hand of the priestly caste. *Priestcraft* twisted Christ's message, erasing crucial facts like reincarnation, all for selfish purposes. It worked too: God-fearing minions are much easier to control! As KH says in the *Mahatma Letters*: 'Ignorance created Gods and cunning took advantage of the opportunity.'"

"I agree, that's a no-brainer, but Naomi–back to my question. I know I'm being dense, but oblige me as a friend: It seems to me even still to be a contradiction: Isn't KH telling a little white lie in the *Aura* book, speaking as if there *is* a personal God, knowing otherwise?"

"Where in that book did you see the words *personal* God? You didn't. Let's retrace: KH is reaching out to a Christian and he knows the almost insurmountable barriers due to a lifetime listening to the scratchy orthodox LP, so– KH lays down a *new* track for the orthodox–by speaking to their soul, by emphasizing *God-like* virtues, *God-like* attributes–never once describing God as a person– but as *electronic light substance*. Think about it: to a Christian mind, what archetype would be worthy enough to contain those divine virtues?"

"A saint? Am I missing something? It still seems a bit like a play on words."

"Jules, look how long it took for *you* to open to them. You, the daughter of an atheist skeptic...I'm sure your Yoga training helped let the Masters into your life. Look at your own case and see the difficulty the Master's face."

"You speak truth, my friend. I was one tough pistachio."

"The Masters know that, they know all. They approach us in a manner suitable, conducive to the heart and soul, compelling."

"Jehovah's witnesses are suitable and compelling?

"Miss pistachio, you are a tough nut to crack–a will of steel. You can't deny that the visit was unforgettable, right?"

"True. If Morya's eyeballs hadn't been so strangely dislodged from his sockets, I might have let the whole incident pass by."

"Faulty! The wise ones would never let that happen, they have their ways *and* their stand-up comedians. Morya is known for his plays on words. This is the first time I have heard of him making a play on his eyes! Are you ready to head in?"

Our host was busy as usual. We found him in his white chef apron, talking on the phone, scheduling reservations 3 months in advance. Straightening the tablecloth, he was simultaneously preparing linen napkins for the morning meal.

"Are you enjoying the grounds, ladies?"

"Absolutely. I am certain that we are being spoiled rotten by the greatest host in the grandest retreat in Shasta!" Naomi wasn't exaggerating: Laundress, maid, head cook and bottle washer, David also offered professional massage services at the historic retreat. I wondered when he found time for his girlfriend.

"May I offer you ladies herbal tea, coffee? Oh, and there are freshly baked muffins and scones from the bakery, if you wish. You ladies let me know if there is anything at all you need."

"David, your reputation precedes you. Thanks, we will let you know if we need anything." The crown moldings, fireplaces and gardens made our stay at the beautifully restored Victorian B&B a truly enchanting one.

"Coup de foudre? I had to look that one up myself," confessed my scholarly friend. I hadn't spoken much French since I cursed the voyeur in Marseilles. A walking encyclopedia, Naomi was good to have around. I asked her for a rendering of the term. "Literally it's a 'bolt of lightning,'" she said, delivering the goods again. "It refers to the *dorje* or *vajra*–the Buddhist's thunderbolt, a symbol of divine power. Figuratively, *coup de foudre* means 'love at first sight.' Qualifies as quite a powerful electric bolt to the system, wouldn't you agree?"

"Would I ever! Strongest power surge I know. I've felt a few love thunderbolts charge through me. I can feel them in my memory body still."

"Isn't love grand? What vitality...what powerful activation."

"Potent stuff. Love affairs are not exclusive to humans. I've told you before of my flower ecstasies, my meditations on trees...all members of the plant kingdom, for that matter."

"It's been a while since we've spent any time together. I wouldn't mind hearing it again."

"I wouldn't mind hearing it again, either! All right, my friend, here it is: Let's use a flower. In the hours before dawn I get the best results. First, I bring to mind a thought of a flower, its natural beauty. I hold it there. I could pick something in the garden blooming, but it's not necessary, as long as I can fix the thought and keep in my mind a lasting image of perfection. I work with colors as you know—some days I need yellow, other times I want blue, sometimes violet, lately aqua. My eyes are closed and I'm focusing with full attention on the flower. I get a strong dose of whatever flower Deva or tree Deva I happen to be invoking. The elemental kingdom has their spirit guides just like we do. So, I have invoked the muse, which drives the spirit to me. My response is automatic, from so many years' love affair with nature. The response comes in the form of prana, which races to my heart and fills me up with ecstasy—at lightning speed. Now, I am flying way out there on the slipstream, rising on a current, riding a natural high of beauty. The song of nature is holding me captive. I've surrendered completely to the elementals' beautiful, tender world, the world of *electronic love-light*. Now my heart is so full that it opens up fully and begins to express itself rhythmically. I begin to whisper poetry, rhythmically. There are rhythm *Muses* in the higher octaves above me, they make themselves known. I feel their presence. They must be the ones helping me compose songs, helping me rhyme. Sometimes I am surprised, coming out with a word I've never used before, sometimes never even *heard* before. After some time in this almost diaphanous, etherial, state of rhythmic poetry *I AM* one with the heights. I am so high that I can no longer speak, I can't compose poetry...That's when I go into the silence. If I have time to stay there, I do. Sometimes I stay in the silence for long periods of time. When I do stay, I am delivered into the 'peace that passeth understanding'–the state that makes itself known because I'm flying or floating somewhere–it doesn't really matter because it's all heavenly. When I fly, I sometimes reach the place of *White Space*, the state of 'no-mind'. It's at these times that I have ascended to the place of the meditating Buddhas–the octave of pure mind, luminous mind. In this high state, I have to work much harder to steady myself, to remain perfectly tuned to the perfection of the pure silence. This requires that I remain perfectly still, focused on the tiniest point in my third eye–the most minimized mantissa... otherwise it is impossible to remain in this octave. As soon as I think *even* one thought while visiting this 'no-mind' state, I am immediately kicked out. With *even* one thought I fall back to earth mind. These space experiments are really fun. I wish everyone would learn to meditate and try them out."

"You know, Jules, for such a rugged mountain woman, you sure have a prominent *fairy* side to you. I'm feeling inspired to give meditation a larger berth in my schedule. You know, I think your flights must have evolved since I last heard, because I don't think I understood that rhythm was so significant."

"For me it is, I can't speak for others. Flowers inspire the poetry. Poetry inspires rhythm. I can't fly without rhythm. That's what gives me the final lift off. Rhythm is the motion that sets my sail without any wind. But the *real* cause behind flying is simple: Flying is powered by *love*. In my case, it's all about love for flowers and trees and birds and music...love for natural beauty. That's what really powers the lift. Nothing can truly fly without *love*."

"So true, so true. For me, sustaining inner stillness is where I need work," Naomi admitted.

"I can't see that flaw in your make-up. You've got us all fooled. Hey,

I don't want to forget to add this: If I have a boyfriend, I add that love to the flower high, making the meditations potent, double-dosed. Now *that* is some really *Big Medicine*. Try using Martin in a meditation. See *only* his perfections, concentrate on those. See what happens."

"I don't know, Jules. You and I are very different. I feel high simply being around certain people. Some souls can inspire me so deeply, I don't want to leave them. I definitely need people around me. I love being with like-minded groups of people."

"The world needs all kinds. I tend to be more of an introvert."

"*You*? An *introvert*? Now that's curious, you're about the warmest friend I know, certainly the easiest to talk to."

"Well, then I'm a *gregarious* introvert who needs lots of solitude. When I'm done interacting with people, I am absolutely done. I've got to quit, split, vamoose. Not with *you* of course, but I can't stand breathing the dank pollution of people's atmospheric cloud."

"You mean their aura, Miss Astrophysicist?"

"Yes, their polluted auras. I no longer enjoy all the friends I did before, I'm having to protect myself more than I used to; I've become too sensitive for most crowds—which can make me sick. You know the mechanics of that science, you're the one who taught me."

"It's true. The initiatic path refines the etheric body; it forges connection to the etheric planes—right on up to our maestros' octaves. Initiations are all different, depending on the needs of the chela. Yours and mine are nothing alike: I'm not so sensitively built. You're a mystic, I'm not. You're musical, I'm not. You've developed your siddhis from Yoga; I don't meditate nearly enough. No, I am content to study the science, to read the Vedic verses, to meditate as often as I can. Theosophy and esoteric philosophies are my true loves. We'll both get there, but through different avenues. Hey! Let's chant the Gayatri Mantra.

"OM BHUR BHUVA SUVAHA
OM TAT SAVITUR VARENYAM
BHARGO DEVASYA DHIMAHI
DHIYO YONAH PRACHODAYAT"

"O, Naomi that is exquisite, so beautiful. Sometimes I remember to chant the Gayatri, but I forget what it means exactly."

"It's Sanskrit for: 'We meditate upon the Cosmic Lord of Light so that That Light of the Soul embraces us and alerts our wills."

"Naomi, you are a treasured encyclopedic resource."

"You flatter me. The Gayatri definition comes from a source I found on the web, *The World Teacher Trust*. Says right here:

'Gayatri, the light of the three worlds, is one of the chief keys of
meditation followed by the Himalayan Aryans from the ancient
most times. Contemplation upon Gayatri is a "Sound and Light
technique" given by the ancient Seers for realization of one's own
etheric form...the five faces of Gayatri carry the five aspects of the
colour, namely the solar light, the lunar light and the colour blue, red
and golden yellow.'

I've been mining this resource–extraordinary writings, Jules. You'd find it very interesting. I'll send you the link to *The World Teacher Trust, WTT*–wonderful minds, these: Obviously in direct contact with the hierarchy and blessed with an enormous cache from their *causal* bodies. These are living Masters, in the flesh, in India. Master KPK, Sri Parvathi Kumar, is giving the world the *Yoga of Synthesis*–building a bridge between East and West. It says:

'Master KPK is a mediator and medium of the Avatar of
Synthesis. His message is synthesis in all fields and on all planes.
He demonstrates to humanity a new form of domestic, economic,
social and spiritual life... If you align your being with The Being,
the work of The Being happens through the being. Such is the state
of an Initiate. He allows himself to be a channel for the Divine

Plan to manifest. The will individual attunes to the Will Divine. Consequently, the Will Divine functions through the individual. "Father, Thy will be done" is the Path of the disciple, the Initiate and the Master."'

"If Kumar is the mediator, who is the *Avatar of Synthesis*?"

"Dr. Ekkirala Krishnamachary–Master EK,who passed in 1984. It says:

'Dr. Ekkirala Krishnamachary, was a university lecturer for Vedic and oriental literature at the Andhra University of Visakhapatnam...He founded numerous spiritual centres in India and Western Europe as well as schools and more than 100 homeopathic dispensaries in India, where the sick are treated for free.'"

"So Master EK was the *Avatar of Synthesis*?"

"Yes, one of them–after *Master CVV,* who transmitted to *Master EK* great insights while he was in meditation. This opened up the Path to Master EK's homeopathic healing work and led to his contact with the Planetary Hierarchy. In 1971 he founded The World Teacher Trust. *Master EK* was a healer of a higher order."

"Don't stop there. Go on."

"You want more goodies? Don't answer that–I know you too well! Since Morya's my teacher and Koot Hoomi is yours, lets' go there. You know how I adore speaking of Morya's lifetime as Thomas More, *"The Man for all Seasons"*–like when he walked up the scaffolding to meet his executioner saying, *"I am the King's good servant, but God's first."* Who do you know that can approach death with such aplomb? Morya's blue ray shines always, but history doesn't often provide us with such tidbits to understand the great ones. In that embodiment Morya's lifelong friend was Erasmus–none other than Koot Hoomi."

"Yes, you mentioned that. What does this have to do with the *Avatar of Synthesis*?"

"Morya and KH incarnated as *Maru*–sometimes written *Moru*–and *Devapi*, at the time of Krishna. They're mentioned in the Vedas, the Puranas and elsewhere–like the Secret Doctrine. You'll love this synopsis: It's taken straight from the *Bhagavatha Scripture* in the 3rd, 9th and 12th cantos:

'At the twilight hours of Dwapara and Kali Yugas, when Lord Krishna was departing from his physical, he initiated Lord Maitreya and installed him as the World Teacher to carry out the Divine Plan for Kali Yuga. Lord Krishna also hinted that he would be ably assisted by others, among whom Maru and Devapi are the chief [Lords].'

"Ever since the time of Krishna, the Divine Plan relating to this earth is to be carried out through Lord Maitreya and his Lords, *Maru* and *Devapi*–*Morya* and *Koot Hoomi*!"

"I feel my body vibrating, Naomi."

"As well you should be: The fact that the Masters have appeared to you in the physical means that you are known to them from past lives. When a world teacher comes to you personally, it means they know they can use you for the *Divine Plan*. You undoubtedly had attainment in past lives. Your flights, to come at such a young age and so naturally–without you even trying...How could you doubt it, with all those *postcards*?"

"I repeat, Naomi, my body is trembling. I need to go to India, to the Himalayas. I want to meet the one directing the WTT. I can *feel* the soul of this work...What did you say the living Master's name is, the voice behind the WTT?"

"Sri Parvathi Kumar, Master KPK. Are you OK? You look a little pale?"

"I need to close my eyes. I'm picking up more magnetism than my puny self can handle at one time. I need to protect myself from total absorption, especially when I'm so receptive like this. Too much truth all at once makes this fairy a little dizzy."

"You're in tune with them, you're a natural synthesizer! Do you want me to stop, Jules?

"No, I'll be fine. Continue, please."

"This part is important because it explains the principles of how *Yoga of Synthesis* relates to Morya's teachings in his *Agni Yoga* books. It says:

'The Yoga of the future is what is called Agni Yoga...Through [the initiate's] discipline of word, thought and deed he trains himself to use the word as the flame of consciousness....From the mental plane to the plane of intelligence we are stepping through the Path of Agni—but in the middle there is the fuel and there is the smoke as the impurity caused by the combustion of fuel in the fire. That is what we call the emotional outbursts....[It is] between the mind and the pure intelligence [that] we have the plane of emotions, which we are expected to cross. The passage of Agni Yoga describes how the disciple crosses this smoky path.'"

"I think I get it: We cross the smoky path by putting thoughts into the flame of Agni for purification before it can reach the emotions—we bypass the emotional body. That reminds me of a recurring vision I had as a child: Paper wads inscribed with vicious words from my siblings immolated themselves into nothingness. It seems to me that by holding the mind steady against the onslaught of malicious words or thoughts—by not reacting to them, but instead purifying them through the fire of Agni—that we are performing a service...a worldwide emotional ecological *Agnification*. We *can* make a difference by purifying the earth's atmosphere from harmful thoughtwaves."

"I like the analogy, Miss Ecologist. Not to jump around, but I want you to hear this before you go off in your reverie, which I can plainly see from your eyes. Attention! Here's Master EK speaking:

'The etheric abode of the Hierarchy is in the Trans-Himalayan caves, and these caves are called the Caves of Kalapa and Sravasti

(Shigatze). Sanat Kumara, the Lord of the planet, is stated to be residing in the etheric around the Gobi Desert. His habitat is known as Shambala. The Divine Plan is conceived from higher circles on a yearly basis during the months of Pisces-Aries in Shambala, and is transmitted to the Hierarchy and to the disciples of the Hierarchy, during the Taurus Full Moon, which is today considered as the Vaisakh Festival. The Plan is further transmitted to the disciples of the Hierarchy, who are working on the physical plane."'

"How long can a tourist stay in Tibet these days, Naomi?"

"I think two weeks, with a tour group, supervised. Are you listening to this?"

"I'm listening, but I'm thinking too. I want to stay in Tibet much longer than two weeks."

"I'm going to sick Morya on you. You once called him "Blueteous Maximus," which I believe you implied meant getting off the duff. Is it fitting *now*–to get you to concentrate on this? You'll get your trip to Tibet. Have patience, my friend."

"I'm listening."

"You're going to love this, Jules: This is about the cycle of Alice Bailey's books through Djwhal Khul. This comes from Krishna's ancient words, how he outlined the plan for the coming age. He speaks of Maitreya, Maru, Devapi and Djwhal Khul:

'I do not make it inevitable that I come down into physical reappearance again and again. It is enough, if I have the soul of an accomplished being as my vehicle. Through that soul, I continue to pervade into the beings. I do this up to the end of the Kali age. I choose your consciousness as the pure vehicle of the present sacrifice of mine. Maru and Devapi continue to pave my way by attracting souls to divine life and give them proper rectification required to get tuned into my presence. From time to time, it is also necessary to galvanize training methods into the fitness of the changing

psychological patterns and also to render the whole pattern of my work approachable and understandable by the people of the various languages through centuries. This part of the work will be taken up by Djwhala Khula under that direction of Maru and Devapi.'"

"Naomi, this is extraordinary."

"OK, now let's go back to Blavatsky and the Theosophical Society. You're getting to know the Maha Chohan better than most, even though you know him as a bird!"

"Morya likes working with birds because birds "get it.""

"True, and witty–even wittier because my witty Master said it. All right, pay attention."

"I'm at your feet, Goddess Saraswati."

"So here's another tie: We know the Maha Chohan was the counselor overseeing establishment of the Theosophical Society, advising KH and M. We learn here on WTT that the Maha Chohan in ancient times was again in a position as counselor–this time to the blind King Dhritarastra in the *Mahabharata*. He was *Mahatma Vidura*–a sage counseling sages! The Maha Chohan is wisdom personified!"

"Blavatsky said he was always frowning."

"I think she may have given him cause to frown. A sage of his experience knows better than to expect too much from a human in a flesh body. Let's hope we can make the Maha Chohan smile this time around. Let's hope we can assist those coming after us."

"I am feeling anxious, Naomi–because he came to me. I was just thinking about being 12 years old, admiring the 'Ruby Glow' *Leptospermum* trees my Dad grew. They were completely covered in ruby blossoms, almost shocking me. I stood there drinking the ruby light–and then a big flash of ruby sent the fire inside me, filling up all the cavities of my body. That must have been the ruby ray electronic light in action! They must be training me in the ruby ray."

"From what I know, ruby is an intense, penetrating laser-like ray–not for the weak of heart."

"You know, Katie boomed at me one time, exclaiming that there was something "*BIG*" I was supposed to do for the saints–scaring me half to death. Man, that woman really could melt me down in an instant. Something shut her up suddenly and she wouldn't say a word more about it. After the volcanic eruption, I sensed she regretted having stepped over the line of scrimmage. Shiza!–that little redhead could pour out a strong dose of *Medicine* from such a tiny mouth. She was always well-meaning, but with her I could find zero *White Space*. Her energy drained me; I never could stay very long."

"Swimming in cold water might have cooled her off the caldera. The Maha Chohan had concerns about women's fire–I mean, when he was Vidura of the *Mahabharata*. Being a woman, I found his words to the King humbling:

'One should not place trust on a woman, a swindler, an idle person, a coward, one that is fierce, one that boasts of his own power, a thief, an ungrateful person, and an atheist.'"

"Naomi, we should get together more often. I just love tapping your big brain. I need some sleep. Oh, and don't forget to be looking for ways I could stay longer than just two weeks in Tibet, OK?

"Oh, go to sleep! No, come to think about, you should read the newest transmission of *The Great Invocation*, the gem from Djwal Khul. I printed this one out from the WTT site. Master D.K.'s prayer will help us both get some deep and rarefied sleep."

THE GREAT INVOCATION

Let us form the Circle of Good Will.

OMNIA VINCIT AMOS

From the South through Love which is pure.
From the West through Wisdom which is true.
From the East through Will which is noble.
From the North through Silence which is golden.
May the Light make beautiful our lives.
O Hierophant of our Rite
Let his love shine.

OMNIA VINCIT AMOS

Let us form the Circle of the World Servers.

We bow down in homage and adoration
To the Glorious and Mighty Hierarchy,
The Inner Government of The World,
and to its Exquisite Jewel,
The Star of the Sea - The World Mother.

From the point of Light within the Mind of God
let Light stream forth into the minds of men.
Let light descend on Earth.

From the point of Love within the Heart of God
let love stream forth into the hearts of men.
May the Lord return to Earth.

From the centre where the Will of God is known
let purpose guide the little wills of men,
the purpose, which the Masters know and serve.

From the centre which we call the race of men
Let the Plan of Love and Light work out
And may it seal the door where evil dwells.

From the Avatar of Synthesis who is around

let His energy pour down in all kingdoms.
May He lift up the Earth to the Kings of Beauty.

The Sons of Men are one and I am one with them.
I seek to love, not hate.
I seek to serve and not exact due service.
I seek to heal, not hurt.

Let pain bring due reward of light and love.
Let the soul control the outer form and life and all events,
and bring to light the love
which underlies the happenings of the time.

Let vision come and insight.
Let the future stand revealed.
Let inner union demonstrate
and outer cleavages be gone.
Let love prevail.
Let all men love.

Master D.K.–Djwal Khul

Chapter 38 Descending Mt. Shasta

The crown of the head is termed the well, because the waves of alien influences penetrate by this way. Everywhere in antiquity we see the covering of the head connected with the symbol of the priest, whereas now this symbol is replaced by the name of a business firm. So men have become spiritually bald!

El Morya

Music is a higher revelation than all wisdom and philosophy. Music is the electrical soil in which spirit lives, thinks and invents

Ludwig van Beethoven

Sun shafts glorified the eastern aspect of the mountain, throwing morning light across the wooded ridges, the giant trees disappearing into the past. Maples and magnificent Firs, the Lodgepole and Western White Pines, Boxelders and oaks– all my new friends were behind us. Having kissed my first Shasta Red Fir, *Abies magnifica var. shastensi*–I shut my eyes, recalling the resin blisters and reddish bark, forwarding to my physical senses the fragrant life essence of the mixed-conifer forest.

"So, Naomi, did you find everything you desired?" I asked, catching the last remnants of the passing *greenness*.

"Absolutely, I just love my new Tibetan singing bowl", my friend said, beaming. "I'm glad Martin reminded me to bring my tuning forks. It sings in *A natural*. I've been looking for a bowl singing in the *indigo* frequencies. I love the sound. It feels like it's my keynote. *Golden Girl*, what does gold correspond to?"

"My *key* is *E*. It's not so much toward the gold as it is to sunshine yellow. Just because it's my *key frequency*–my major soul correspondence–it doesn't make it my *keynote*. As I understand it, the *keynote* can reflect the *key* of your soul—but it's not the same thing at all. The *keynote* has more to do with the expression, the emphasis, tempo, the mood through the melody and score—it's what best describes that one unique snowflake of our individuality. Take Morya, for example: As you know, his *keynote* is Elgar's *Pomp and Circumstance No. 1*, the song that used to make us cry when they crowned the *Queen for a Day* on TV. Anyway, that's in the key of *D major*, the orange range—definitely *not* Morya's ray. His is the *key of blue*. Blue frequencies correspond to the *G chord*."

"I should have studied piano. My parents insisted I take up the violin at a very young age. Bad decision. I had no love for the thing and never took up another instrument because of the negative experience."

"Naomi, don't let that old memory contaminate your appreciation for the violin! Don't let anything limit you. Which reminds me, I didn't finish about non-limitations: Even though I am composed predominantly of the yellow ray, I don't limit myself to the yellow of the *Love-Wisdom Ray*. I work with all tones that strike a chord inside me—although I do have my favorites. I'm conducting a little frequency experiment to see what *frequency-vitamin* I need for each day. What I do is simple: I composed a piano song which I transpose to different keys. When I play the song in different keys, I pay attention to the feelings resounding through my body's soundboard. For me, it works best to play with my eyes closed, to just *feel* the color. It seemed to me an easy and fun way to find my *ray* requirement *du jour*."

"I won't be able to make a color-tone *du jour* in this embodiment, I'm afraid. I'll stick to just listening to the great ones play, but I will make it a habit now to check the correspondence."

"I wish you had been there with me to hear Yevgeny Sudbin play Chopin's *Fantasie in F minor*, I thought my heart would burst, I cried like a baby."

"Chopin is rather intimate, isn't he?"

"Sudbin is too! He's our new "Russian Chopin," incredible young artist. Re-creating Chopin's delicate style takes enormous talent, a daunting challenge for even the greatest pianists. I read that Chopin was very fragile–so ill that his later masterpieces reflect this physical infirmity–by way of their incredible delicacy. Poor thing was so sickly his last years, but even illness can't hide that depth of genius. Chopin's *legatos* can only be played from the heart fire, otherwise they lack his authenticity. Green is the color of the heart chakra and you can't fake the feeling of the heart. You can tell if the performer is tuned to the heart of those immortal legatos. *Fantasie in F minor* is in the heart's *key of green*. Sudbin played with Chopin's *green-heart* delicacy, in *mega-kleenex sympatico.*"

"*Mega-kleenex sympatico?* You do love to play with words, Jules."

"Words...music...colors...plants–these are my toys, great fun. I've been playing with violet toys recently. I have a *B-tone* Tibetan singing bowl, in the *violet* range–it makes me *feel* like I'm ascending, something magic about *B chords. B* minor is very healing to me right now, or as my Apache friend might say–*Big B Medicine.*"

"So, I gather this weekend met your expectations, Jules?"

"Met and exceeded. To discover that my father and I have been on the same radio frequency all this time, following the same wisdom teaching. When he finds out that his beloved Krishnamurti was Koot Hoomi's chela–I want to see his reaction. I'll be sailing for some time on that one. To be able to tell my "atheist" father that we've been following the same path all along–that my teacher is his teacher's teacher! –now *that* is a grand slam home run!"

"I see you are building your own *Little Alexandria,* girl! How many books did you end up with?"

"Eleven and a-half, counting the Édouard Schuré pamphlet. Well, not really a pamphlet, just that the publisher uses a huge pica and blank pages to make up for lack of volume–to me, that seems a bit sketchy."

"Too bad they didn't have Schuré's out-of-print *Great Initiates,* combining all the greats. That's a fabulous work–a *must read* for you sometime down the line."

"The cerebral clerk was devouring Schuré's *Orpheus.* I need to focus on the Maha Chohan in his life as Orpheus. I've never come across any book on Orpheus. My knowledge quest is definitely in its infancy, I'm afraid: Orpheus was in my head as a mythical archetype."

 "You're not alone; the world is fed on myth as fiction, yet myths are often truths embodied in story. Jung brought us closer to the great archetypes through dream. I'm sure Jung knew much more about the mythic heroes and heroines than he let on."

" Name some "mythical" heroes that are real."

"Hercules was real. You know that, right?"

"No, I did not. Educate me, please Naomi."

"*Hercules' Labors* are accounts of his earth life. His supreme efforts in the 12 labors are what earned him his ascension. Hercules endured every one of the hardships that were given to him and when he died he was delivered to Mount Olympus–on a chariot no less–to live with the gods. Brought forward to the present, *Hercules' Labors* would represent a "pilgrim on the initiatic path to progress" as Adrian would put it. Hercules labored unceasingly to throw off his karmic gravity, but that wasn't enough: He still had to shed the mortal vehicle, the ego–the dweller on the threshold. The ego is what blinds man, keeps him from reaching his highest attainments."

"You are speaking of the divine principles–*Atma-Buddhi*? That he learned to use these principles, rather than the egoic license of the senses that want to control the body?"

"Yes, the five senses typically are in control of man, who stands to lose everything of value in this delusional state. It's a very poor state of the union, I might add."

"Naomi, I have to admit: I'm having a problem swallowing that pill that Hercules was a real person. It makes my puny little rational brain want to implode."

"Then don't use your rational brain! Use your *divine* intuition–your *Buddhic* mind–as you know you are quite capable of doing. Forget what we learned about Hercules from the textbooks–the authors are woefully mistaken. As bizarre as it sounds, Hercules incarnated as a human being and worked his way back to Mount Olympus. He acts now as the Elohim of the blue ray, the ray of divine will. He is one of Morya's mentors! Step outside your old paradigm, girlfriend."

"My father could never accept this; I would not dare speak of this to him."

"You mean his *rational* brain could not accept this. I find it helpful to go back to the simple teaching of Gautama Buddha, the father of all adepts, who said something like: to learn the highest wisdom, you must make room for the truth–meaning, forget everything you have ever learned. Conventional "wisdom" is ignorant– biased opinions and half-truths. We must clean our mental houses, especially the upper stories! Now, aren't I clever? Jules, with your Yoga you already know the techniques to cleanse your mind from useless clutter."

"Naomi, can you give me five minutes of silence, please? I need to turn my piggy bank upside down...I want to empty some useless shiny pennies I've been saving. I'll be with you momentarily."

Wending our way downhill, the view of the Cascades receded into the past behind us, but the bond with Shasta Mountain had not. The taste of forest dew was still on my tongue. At intervals, pine resin I had wiped on my jeans sent wafts up my nostrils, making the mountain pull on my heart strings like a sweet Shakespearean parting. A surge of gratitude pulsed through my body in waves, musing–not solely on the sylvan delights of Shasta–but also on the delightful and brilliant soul behind the wheel next to me. In the passenger seat, I was free to contemplate the atoms that were quickening and whirling inside of me. Turning my thoughts north,

I pondered the last 48 hours on the mountain.

"Naomi, please continue what you were saying about GMOs," I requested of my friend, breaking the long silence. "What are they doing in their *Frankenfood* labs these days?"

"Look in the back seat, there's a purple folder. I printed out Matin's email, a rough outline–raw research. Martin likes to hear my thoughts so I brought it along in case I had a moment. Brace yourself, my dear–you are *not* going to like what you read."

Pulling out the notes I read the heading: "*GMOs-The March of the Silent, but Deadly Foe.*" The rawness of the notes spoke candidly of how the "rich-and-getting-richer-by-the-minute" GMO corporations are systematically poisoning not only our food supply, but are committing atrocities and grievous crimes against nature–most recently the bees–man's best friends–who have been dying off in droves. 'One third of the world's honeybees have been killed off from GMOs...Honeybees are fed genetically-modified HFCS (high fructose corn syrup). Bees feeding on GM pollen are dying, collapsing from cancer of the digestive tract disease, e.g. colorectal cancer. *Colony Collapse Disorder* is linked to the unfortunate fact that our bees are feeding on contaminated GM pollen in the course of their natural service to life: pollination, dying off from the poisonous pollen of GM-modified crops.'

I read further: 'GMO corporations have created seeds that reproduce only under certain conditions, often linked to the use of their own brands of fertilizer and/or insecticide. These seeds are genetically engineered to produce only infertile seeds, which farmers cannot replant. Bees that are trying to collect pollen, are found to have digestive tract diseases, such as amoeba and nosema disease. After studies of the autopsy, the most alarming trait is that the lower intestine and stinger show discoloration to solid black versus the normal opaque color, discoloration as is typically seen in cases of human colon cancer.'

'Half to three-fourths of a million bee colonies have died. This is no urban legend. It is serious. 2007 Mid-Atlantic Apiculture Research and Extension Consortium's Colony Collapse Syndrome Disorder Working Group.'

Martin's raw notes–replete with scientific facts and overwhelming evidence from the test results of esteemed scientists'–link GMO consumption to various cancers and diseases such as pancreatic, liver, thyroid, hormonal and immune-system malfunctions. Eminent European scientists from several different countries were quickly removed from their tenured positions immediately after reporting their critical findings.'

I was sick to my stomach reading of the wholesale contamination of our precious resources, the unconscionable health threat to humanity–reeling from the vicious assaults on the innocent nature kingdom. The frightening list of GM experiments made me almost bilious. They have ugly plans for our future:

* Corn engineered with human genes
* Sugarcane engineered with human genes
* Rice engineered with human genes
* Human genes inserted into corn to produce spermicide
* Corn engineered with hepatitis virus genes
* Spider genes into goat DNA for use in bulletproof vests.
* Corn engineered with jellyfish genes
* Jellyfish genes injected into pigs to light up pigs' noses in the dark
* Arctic fish genes injected into tomatoes and strawberries for frost tolerance
* Potatoes injected with GMOs to glow in the dark for irrigation efficiency

*   Tobacco engineered using lettuce genes

Martin's notes pressed hard on my heart valves, throwing my heart into overdrive; the painful sense of urgency signaled the dire truth: **Nature and natural law–of man, beast and plant life–is being usurped–worldwide–by maniacal mercenaries, marketing themselves as technology's future heroes**. Any rational personal who looks squarely at the facts–any sentient being having any ethics at all–will see the GM scoundrels in their true light: *The GMO corporations are less-than-human, scheming tacticians–banking on corporate return alone.* The greed of the military-industrial complex is at hand and it is raging all across the world.

Claims of safety? B.S.! The EU's numerous, independent tests show unequivocally the GM-corporate "safety first" claims to be preposterous lies. Under penalty of legal action, scientists are forced to use "politically correct" phrasing in public–but their test results *do not lie*. The scientists posses a legal weapon: Their scientific facts prove that GMOs pose a *real and present danger* to human health and the environment. Who stands to gain from all this maneuvering? Just look at the recent news: The top GMO legal hit-man has been elevated to the top post at the U.S.-FDA, the agency ultimately responsible for approving or denying which poisonous additives end up in our food supply! The fox has been invited–officially–into the henhouse.

Europe's scientific body reports: 'We can conclude, from the regulatory tests performed today, that it is unacceptable to submit 500 million Europeans and several bilions of consumers worldwide to the new pesticide GM-derived foods or feed, this being done without more controls (if any) than the 3-month-long toxicological tests and using only one mammalian species, especially since there is growing evidence of concern. <u>There is no epidemiological follow-up for lack of traceability and labeling in GM-producing American countries.</u>'

While the U.S. Dept. of Pesticide Regulation requires 2 years for toxicology screening for pesticides, GM plants require only 3 months of testing! Yet GMOs not only embody pesticides, *GMOs produce pesticides.*

'The Cartagena Biosafety Protocol identifying GMOs at the borders of a country has now been signed by over 150 countries, including the member states of the European Union...Countries, which so far do not follow the process-based approach to biosafety legislation, are the USA and Canada.'

Reading Martin's notes *in toto,* I was seized by a repulsion so strong I jerked at the window, rolling it down all the way, needing to cool my jets. Looking at the pristine beauty of nature all around me, and having slept the past nights surrounded by one of the great forests of antiquity–I fantasized myself personally handcuffing every last one of the S-O-Bs–locking them up for a life sentence *before* they sentence the planet to a GMO-poison death. Asking myself how it was possible that the world has allowed this monster such a stronghold, the image appeared in my mind–flashing as a giant sociopathic genocide. Silently branding the ignorant bastards, I chose not to share with Naomi the monikers churning in my mind, condemning them further.

With my head out the window, the fresh air took me to new avenues of thought: In solemn gratitude for my father's wisdom, I sat back in silence–recalling my father's strict prohibition, refusing to feed his children *all* processed food. Even back then he warned us vehemently of food additives not fit for consumption: All processed food was *Pizon.*

Requesting silence, I said a prayer for the beautiful bees. Weeping, I made a long prayer for mankind, wondering who had the wisdom to stand in the place of my father. Who would be there to watch over the next generation of children?

Chapter 39 The Mahatma Letters

'We do not bow our heads in the dust before the mystery of mind—for we have solved it ages ago... We believe in <u>Matter</u> alone, in matter as visible nature and matter in its invisibility as the invisible, omnipresent, omnipotent Proteus with its unceasing motion which is its life, and which nature draws from herself since she is the great whole outside of which nothing can exist.'

'...Your science knows less than one of our Tibetan Yak-drivers of Kant's metaphysics.'

Mahatma Letters, K.H. to A.P. Sinnett No.X, 1881

How many times, having started out for Egypt, have We found Ourselves in Mongolia? How many times, having found a manuscript, have We locked it up again?

One should not hesitate. Walk like lions! Righteousness adorns your armor.

El Morya

Shasta was the perfect antidote to my confused collection of ideas, ideas taken from too many sources—too many ideas tweaked by varying levels of insight. Coming back to my hill, I relished my new books that were written from deeper levels of understanding: treasures penned by initiated sages. The signature memento standing head and shoulders above the rest was one book. Swiftly correcting my clouded perceptions was *The Mahatma Letters—KH's Big Medicine*—just what the doctor ordered. Deserted on an island with nothing other than *The Mahatma Letters*— I could still count myself lucky. The *Letters*, written by the hands of KH and his dearest friend and fellow adept, Morya, were for me that priceless treasure at long last: I was in direct contact with my wise Master's precision mind; unadulterated, authentic. I could feel KH's vibrations through the cadence of the heart-hand-music, through the rhythm of his syntax. This time my preceptor's voice was not conveyed through an amanuensis: This was his very own voice, a voice steeped in the ancient science. KH was a Master of the ancient wisdom– the voice of Theosophy.

Corresponding from *Shigatze, Tibet*, KH's linguistic skill and dry wit in the *Letters* paint an intimate picture of the adept as he wends his way through the frustrating ordeal: transferring obscure Buddhistic cosmology to his uninitiated, British correspondent in Simla, India. Known for his "sublime philosophical and ethical instruction" KH's goal was to establish an Anglo-Indian branch of the Theosophical Society (TS), and in the process steer the British from entrenched falsehoods, such as the Spiritualist movement then raging in London. KH's correspondent, A.P. Sinnett, an editor of a highly influential Indian newspaper, was well educated and enthusiastic–but narrow minded and uninitiated. The goal of "Brotherhood" being a sticking point for the arrogant British, KH's comment drives the point home:

"...the majority of our Anglo-Indians, among whom the terms 'Hindu' or 'Asiatic' is generally coupled with a vague yet actual idea of one who uses his fingers instead of a bit of cambric, and who abjures soap–would most certainly prefer an American to 'a greasy Tibetan.'

Fortunately for me, KH must constantly invent ways to instruct the uninitiated Sinnett, repeating his instruction from various angles. *The Mahatma Letters* granted me a crisp understanding of the cosmos from the perception of the "greatest adept that ever lived"–Siddhartha or Guatama Buddha. The *Letters* solved a personal dilemma for me: What was the precise reasoning behind my father's atheist arguments against the existence of God? Both my father and KH spoke through one mind, that of the Buddha– who saw clearly while in the highest Nirvanic states–that the universe is governed not by a being, but by natural laws–laws of causes and effects.

Quite distinct from the personal 'God' of the Christians, KH explains in the *Letters–*

'Our philosophy falls under the definition of Hobbes. It is preeminently the science of effects by their causes, and of causes by their effects...It either affirms or denies, for it never teaches but that which it knows to be the truth...Parabrahm is not a god, but absolute immutable law, and Iswar is the effect of Avidya and Maya, ignorance based upon the great delusion.... The God of the Theologians is simply an imaginary power, *un loup garou* as d'Holbach expressed it–a power which has never yet manifested itself. Our chief aim is to deliver humanity of this nightmare, to teach man virtue for it's own sake, and to walk in life relying on himself instead of leaning on a theological crutch that for countless ages was the direct cause of nearly all human misery.'

Again KH explains the fallacy:

'...who but a Theologian nursed on mystery and the most absurd supernaturalism can imagine a self existent being of necessity infinite and omnipresent *outside* the manifested *boundless* universe... When we speak of our *One Life* we also say that it penetrates, nay is the *essence* of every atom of matter; and that therefore it not only has correspondence with matter but has all its properties likewise, etc.– hence *is* material, is *matter itself.*'

Pondering the ideas of my Native American friends, Adrian and Katie, I saw how closely they matched those of the theosophists– *Great Spirit* of the Native Americans and *Parabrahm* appeared to be near equivalents.

Chapter 40   The Antahkarana

One must speak about those who oppose and threaten Me. It is light-minded to hope that a rent in the web of the world can be easily mended. Even a simple sound may bring an unexpected echo from afar. How much deeper does the sending of the spirit pierce into space! And these wounds are almost unhealable.

The scientist who forgets about the Source deprives himself of flights into the domain of higher conquests. Children will grasp this simple condition, but many adults reject it as nonsense.

El Morya

Plunging into the lives of the great theosophists unabated, I poured my life into the minds of the *Great Initiates*: Krishna and Orpheus, Hermes and Plato, Rama and Moses, Pythagoras, Jesus and Buddha. Every last erg of mental energy I saved for the endeavor, making a personal philosophical overhaul–a major upgrade from the half-baked paradigms of old. Each day opened out a wider vista, taking me across borders I thought I had already crossed, humbling me in the process. The more I read, the more I realized how little I knew. Soaring into the fastnesses of space had not explained much. On the contrary–my flights only brought more questions, more unexplained phenomena. When finally *The Mahatma Letters* entered my library and my life, the Master's own words woke me up. Studying KH's soul through his letters I understood something of the genius of Pythagoras–one of his previous incarnations. Feeling his sweetness through the *Letters*, it was not difficult discerning the soul of St. Francis–another of his past embodiments. Understanding more of his solemn devotion to truth explained his embodiment as Saint Bernard of Clairvaux.

Humbled by the greatness of His soul, my own fruit was beginning to ripen– simply by being in close contact with His radiance: the burgeoning of my own soul music was learning to dance in spirit.

In this new light of understanding, I made myself ready, at last offering myself up to KH in a Master-chela relationship, offering the light of my aura for His use in times of planetary need.

My Kriya practice had reached new heights by this juncture, becoming exquisite and deep. In the peaceful shelter of Kriya meditation, I could escape the mind-rattling currents and deafening sound bytes of worldly events. Turning my thoughts away from the world, I learned to walk between the two worlds: that of man, and that of the etheric retreat of my Master– in the octaves above Shigatze, Tibet where, in his last incarnation he left his immortal imprints, magnetizing the location for later use. Magnetizing retreats goes something like this: Using electronic light the Masters embed ineradicable forcefields–or "faithfields," as Morya calls them–in which to draw chelas of their spectral band. Those who have been awakened to the hierarchal voices are summoned for a probationary period which, after proving themselves able they graduate through a series of lessons called initiations. Those on the Yellow Ray, such as myself, are mentored under Masters of the Second ray, the Yellow Ray of *Love-Wisdom*.

With my new library and several teachers looking over my shoulder, I now possessed everything I would ever need in this lifetime. Now in the firm hands of the Masters of wisdom, I learned something of the supermundane worlds from my *supermen* friends–those of the *Brotherhood*, who had achieved far superior attainment than what is possible on this physical plane. I was being given an inner knowledge of outer space, the cosmological fastnesses of which have been known for long ages by the ancients of India, who rediscovered the secrets while alone in meditation in forests and Himalayan peaks.

In training the mind to focus *not* on the false specters driving the earth to madness–but on the rarified realms of perfection, a chela is given tools: Using the omnipresent electronic light rays, the chela learns the art of shielding the heart and mind from the poisonous arrows of negative thought forms, which dark clouds contaminate the earth's atmosphere. The chela keeps the attention centered on virtuous qualities, choosing relationship with those mutually supportive of the cause of good will to all, peace and harmony under all circumstances–not an easy feat! Choosing peace at each opportunity, the goal over time is to achieve perfect self-control, restraining the *five horses of sense.* Underlying the chela's development is his own willpower:

'To be or not to be? That is the question.'

Initiations require much discipline. The initiates' body becomes exquisitely sensitive due to the nature of the finer sheaths which absorb light substance– undergoing an "electronic light body-building" process– resulting in increased light in the finer bodies. The Brotherhood looks for bodies of light on earth, their plan being to create electronic light-fields in as many locations as possible, using their chelas to magnetize the earth for purposes of our evolution. The earth is enduring birthing pains, explains the Maha Chohan in *Electrons and the Elemental Kingdom*–adjusting itself to the imbalances produced by humanity's errors, through ignorance.

I must confess: It took me a while to adjust to the idea of communicating with invisible beings. As a result of this new paradigm-shift, my friendships changed: out with the old and in with the new. I could share with only a handful of friends my personal communiqués with Master KH. It was easier to keep silent than to launch into explanations to the uninitiated, to those who never did catch on to the reality of the Saints, who didn't want to know too much about the ascension and who didn't seem to care that it was mankind's evolutionary goal. Ah, I sighed…my friends had not experienced flight, so how could they be expected to dial in to such seemingly distant possibilities? I gave up trying to explain the feeling I got when in high states of meditation. I gave up trying to explain the exhilaration of passing all the way through a pink tunnel at warp speed or soaring through the galaxy to distant stars.

It was too embarrassing to share with uninitiated friends my flight down to the center of the earth! Yes, the center of the earth is where I was guided one night while following a ruby-colored star that I beheld through my third eye while in meditation: Moving effortlessly through the air at high speed, I came into a warp. I couldn't *feel* myself moving, but could *hear* my movement and *see* that I was flying as I passed by a multitude of stars. When I saw patches of filamentous algae passing by me, I realized that I was now moving through water. Soon thereafter, I beheld a loving Buddha who, with both hands—one-at-a-time—emitted electronic ruby ray light from his chest: Gathering ruby light from his heart, the Buddha distributed his light out into the atmosphere. It was here that I also beheld the *Great Central Sun of Even Pressure*. Yes, there is a sun in the center of the Earth— *I know because I was there.*

My space explorations did not make for good "coffee talk," the conversations might get mixed up with the popular ETs raging on TV and film. 'Yes, yes, I would say—the endless cases of ET sightings, both personal and military documentations, cannot be dismissed. Who cares? What's the big deal? ETs have never harmed us. On the contrary, it is us earthlings who pose danger to extraterrestrials! Don't forget Hiroshima!' What mindless person can believe we have not affected distant parts of the cosmos? What fool believes we are an isolated species? Only the ignorant embrace such thoughts— only the uninitiated. 'Read the books,' I would say to them, offering to loan books from my own library for my friends' edification. 'I don't have time' they would answer.

The adept and the mystic can see that the cosmos is united across a giant morphic field— as did the blind man who, when sighted by Jesus exclaimed: "I see men as trees walking"—this being Sephirotic symbolism—that each individual monad or Oversoul has an individualized *Tree of Life*, a sacred grid of electronic light housing the morphic field which in turn contains the human aura. How can science correctly theorize when they have not yet discovered the aura of the *Great Central Sun– the First Cause*–which permeates the entire cosmic egg and from which fire we owe our little spark?

Master Morya regards the current superstring theorists this way: He says the theory is faulty, being based on a perceptual reality *outside* of the unity field of the *Antahkarana* matrix–the web of life permeating all planes of being. All life is of one source, connected at an energetic level within a divine field of living, fluidic light substance. Morya says that unless scientists perceive the existence of a supernal creative being, the divine essence that is the cause of all that is, they may never reconcile all the equations of the universe. The *Antahkarana* matrix indicates that the whole of the universe is a conscious, living, feeling and breathing being–a sentient totality.

The Masters' octave vibrates at a very high frequency, a very high state of consciousness. With sound and thought pollution down here on earth, it is no wonder we don't hear their messages– they can't get through to us! Earthlings' habitat is one of low frequency–a state of anxiety fixated by violence and chaos. After the TV and video games, into the mouth comes the joint, the Chardonnay or the pill–self-medicating the aching soul who is crying out for solace from the onslaught of horror. Victimized, the soul is beyond reception, forced into stupefaction–into unconsciousness where the Master's voice is muted.

If earthlings would dare to turn off the news and 'turn on' to the pranic highs in nature, their sensitivity would return– much like children who, in their innocence, naturally sense the stirrings of the invisible, *natural* world. If we could quiet our souls long enough we would hear the Masters calling to us. Instead of dirty bong water, the path of initiation is a clean, *natural* high worth exploring. Light a candle and dial in to the frequencies of the Saints who are ready to take your calls 24/7. The initiatic path is the way to bypass the trip to the lower heavens, the *Devachan*–reserved for those still clinging to material earth life, and to instead enter the ascended Master octave. Sincere heart and humility are requirements before a Master is lawfully able to take on the responsibility of a *chela*. The laws of conservation of energy are in effect: None shall be wasted.

The chela must be ready for class or else fail the tests. Self-correction is a good thing; I had many lessons to learn. Debris clouded my focus. With mental and emotional detritus clogging the pipeline, I was blind-sighted or, as Master St. Germain says: "We see through a glass darkly." KH gave me gentle warnings, in the form of songs, telling me of the homework I had ahead of me: my pride. Pride, I learned, doesn't really "go before the fall," pride *is* the fall. Until I could begin the painful process of self-correction, I would remain languishing in false perceptions of myself, the very thing I wanted to correct. Until I could see myself in action I could not make the needed self-correction. Struggling with my lower quaternary–the animal nature–in its forceful presentation of maximum resistance– the ego fights back. Catching the milk before it spills is like learning how to live all over again; no Teacher ever claimed it was easy. Once across the Rubicon though, you never look back. Yet all the while– even though my upper triad was winning– I had to be reminded more than a few times that marching forward through this earthly life, I would always be a work in progress.

We often are our own worst enemy. My mind–being mercurial– had been free too long, behaving much like a radio toy seek-and-scan device. Add to that, a highly sensitive ear, such that dissonant sounds and shrill voices disturbed me. Add to that my stubborn and independent nature. Add to that my skepticism, my rigid *terra firma*, no matter what the source–and one might say that I carried a shield of "armed resistance." I was a soul lacking in self-discipline *and* full of independent spirit– a "tough sell."

To say I was a handful is too conservative: It took the Masters more than a little nudge: It took a call from Jehovah's Witnesses, a bowing Swan Dove, a white feather that perfumed my truck for a month, KH's mysteriously-appearing book, and a self-illuminating Starling– to get my full attention and my fealty. None of my philosopher friends had ever heard of anyone being visited by human-eyed birds, angelic whisperings and chanting monks, nor of being approached by the Masters in a physical body–a simple feat for them, but a rare one. The Masters literally had to knock on my door to get my attention!

A word of warning: The unwary, inexperienced traveler must use good sense and caution. Without a proper guide the invisible realms can be downright perilous, leaving more than a few pilgrims unbalanced after a headfirst dive into the arms of a false teacher. The teachings all say to avoid–like poison–trance channelers who, in that state, haven't a clue who is speaking through them. The Masters warn that trance channeling leads to evil karma, both for the medium as well as his patron; that channeling is viable only through a fully conscious, fully trained initiate. More than a few earn their living on their arts of deception, and many are the innocents who become victimized by the sleight-of-hand impostures. The warehouse doors of New Age *misinformation* are wide open; Neptunian delusion floats freely down river. Pilgrim beware! Too few take the time to discern between fact and fiction, paying little or no heed to the wisdom: *Test the teacher behind his message.* Negative forces would desire nothing more than to trip up the traveler, dissuading him from the path to truth.

In this unfamiliar, strange and cloudy atmosphere, I used my own brand of testing. Into my crucible went certain requisite tests: I required of KH bonified proofs *before* I would accept his revelations. For instance, I required proof that I had indeed received the message correctly– that it came from KH and *not* from my own lower self– a common mistake for pilgrims who want so badly to believe a thing is true rather than testing its validity. I found it helpful to demand that KH use *only* words not already in my lexicon, words I never used or rarely heard, reasoning it was a good test to confirm the idea had not come from my own mind. This test had an unforeseen advantage: racing to my Macintosh to look up definitions added a notable increase to my vocabulary.

Chapter 41   Twin Rays

*There is no past, there is the light of the future—by it walk! I
summoned you from the gulf of life....I sharpened your teeth. I set
before you the color of the banner. Understand the Teaching with
a full sweep of wings....Ascend by the most valiant thoughts, for I
have lifted the flap of your tent with lightning. In spirit forget about
insignificance. The predestined Light is great. So walk!*

El Morya

My parents passed from the earth plane within six months of
each other, my father first—leaving us just days before his 86th
birthday. I had heard about this phenomenon occurring to pairs
whose cemented bonds are suddenly severed after, in this case—65
years of marriage. It would seem as though life is not worth living
without that warm, life-giving bond, without having your true love
next to you. Heaven knows I cried a river for them both, precious
as they were to me, reeling from the emptiness that followed the
wake of their departure. I had lost my two best friends; friends
utterly impossible to replace in one short lifetime.

Thankfully, I had the foresight to spend a full year with them down
in San Diego before their passing, wanting to make their life as
fulfilled as it could be under the circumstances of aging which,
for my beautiful Mother was not difficult—taking it all in stride in
Mother's calm and peaceful way. My Father was a different story:
With his masculine pride the realities of aging were for him a tough
pill to swallow—they didn't go down as gracefully.

Spending the year with my parents in the warm southland of San
Diego, I continued my daily Kriya Yoga meditations. Locating a
comfy chair in the wildlands behind their house, I made a semi-
permanent private blind behind the Sumacs. Holding vigil for my
parents and for myself—knowing it was only too soon for the loss—I
soon began to receive visions, some of them of beautiful birds which,

I surmised, my parents would soon come to see in the afterlife. Through the years, it was at my most stressful moments when divine visions had come to my side and this stressful time was no exception. Etheric flashes were followed by flocks of otherworldly birds–magnificent white flyers–whose ornithological origins were quite beyond any worldly kin. On one occasion I observed earthly birds performing unusual math demonstrations before me–flying in perfect geometrical patterns. These common sparrows made not-so-common flight rotations–forming repeated patterns in a large sphere. After each full rotation around the sphere the total number of birds in the sequence would change–the "absent" bird or birds disappearing mysteriously in the Sumac scrub. It dawned on me that I was watching a mathematical display, in geometric symbolism of the alchemical magic of the number five. Even though I could not fully understand the symbolism, it was a charming display nonetheless. Perhaps the fantastic avian display will be of use to me sometime in the future.

Early one evening, just back from joining my Father and his Pomeranian, "Puff," on our twice-daily walk, I lay down on my bed, trying hard to think about something other than the pending loss of such precious friends. Feeling the depth of my loneliness, I lost myself in thought, staring up at the ceiling at nothing in particular. In calm contemplation, I lightly closed my eyelids but remained fully conscious–for how many minutes I remained in this reverie I can't say.

What I can say is that a surprise miracle orgasm came down and blessed me! How does one describe having an orgasm when the male source is operating from the heaven world? That is exactly what happened. Along with my climax came a sound that I don't know how to describe exactly: Imagine being underwater in a submarine and think of the strange sounds that harken from the deep. Now add to that a cooling sensation followed by a breeze arriving with a different sound–somewhere between a whispering willow and a million locusts buzzing. In total surrender I simply lay still on the bed, listening for anything more that was to be delivered from this lovely *organic postcard*–wondering what to make of the "immaculate" arousal, awaiting my throbbing *ku-ku* to release its final, unsolicited quiver. If not the longest ecstatic moment in my life, it was certainly the most memorable. Truly I could now say, along with Ed Sullivan:"*Tonight, we have a really* **BIG** *show.*" That is what I thought that remarkable evening, wondering who it was I had hosted on my bedroom stage.

Alone in the Sumac wildlands above my parents' home–everything was made clear to me: I had been introduced–in a racy kind of way–to my *Twin Ray*, the other half of me who had ascended before me. My *Twin* is waiting for my return to the etheric octaves at the close of this lifetime. What an ecstatic introduction!

A *Twin Ray*, or *Twin Flame* is exciting news for us all: Described as our other half, our essential nature as a whole being includes another. From one perfected whole each of us divided into two equal, but opposite, polarities after our original *ideation*. From *Man*, *Womb-Man* emerged as his complement. Although we experience the cyclic rounds of existence as two halves, once we have ascended–we merge with our original Solar Presence–our personal "First Cause." After that final merging, we are reunited forever. *Twin Rays* are mirror-images of each other: the patterns are identical, though in polarity. When this divine fusion takes place, a *doubling of the Buddhic state* causes a cosmic explosion of light– fohatic light of alchemical reunion.

If you've experienced strange events and "postcards from the edge"–don't worry, be happy: It may mean your Twin Ray is calling you home, getting you ready for graduation from the Earth plane. The breaking news is that, being on Earth with your twin already ascended, you have much more power at your conscious command: Combining prayers with your Twin Ray, there is now the potential for a quadrupling effect of power to factor into the equation. I presume this to be the result of the perfect correspondence in the Twin Ray's electronic light bodies now consciously merging. Another way I look at it is this: By using the "talents" accumulated in our *causal* body, we can deliver the full momentum of not merely our *own* causal body, but the combined energies of both Twin Rays. Not only are Twin Rays four times more powerful than a single flame, according to Morya they "create multidimensionally and may fuse spirit with matter."

Epilogue

With my heart set in eagerness, I followed the trail of my Teacher, KH. There were indeed times when Morya's blue ray descended to admonish me with a more forceful hand, changing my course slightly across the uncharted–but exalted–waters known so well by the Masters of Wisdom. Meditating with the Masters' images in focus, I carried on diligently, earnestly–and in time I would gain that keenness of the ear that knows the Master's voice from a simple whispering in the treetops. Tender sensitivity towards all of nature: the greens of earth, man and beast– grew inside me, requiring of me an allotment of solitude more than ever before. Dissonant voices and loud music became utterly objectionable, jarring to my now highly sensitized system; certain auras I found to stifle even my breath.

Over the course of a decade my chela-ship would take me through my past. I was presented with 33 of my past embodiments–scanning all the way back to Vedic times, to the times of Krishna, the Hindu Christ. Peeking into the past at numerous embodiments in India with both Morya and Koot Hoomi– and again in Assisi and Japan with KH– it was no longer a curious wonder that they felt so like my family. Learning of embodiments in Greece and elsewhere with my "Swan-Dove" threw light on my past associations with the Maha Chohan, who had known me before. Discovering that I had funded Christopher Columbus' expeditions brought the memory of St.Germain's eyes to the present–those of an old friend that I knew– not only as the Catholic Isabella of Spain, but in several lifetimes previous.

Perhaps the most striking gift was the discovery that would erase the tired notions I held about my sister, the *"Mallard."* My sister had earned the highest respect from Morya back in ancient India when she held a top post under his reign. It was due to my sister's unparalleled genius that Morya was able to unify India into one kingdom: Without her genius, Morya's ancient kingdom would not have achieved the Herculean success it did.

Among the lifetimes of my father, I learned it was *"Monsieur Greeners"* himself whose penetrating thoughts as René Descartes gave us the *Cartesian coordinates* and made famous the axiom: *"I think, therefore I AM"*.

Looking into the past brought me more firmly into the present, realizing that life is too short for quarrels and holding onto grievances. Forgiveness is the foremost task for a chela on the path of initiation. Learning to forgive lifts the burden of weight off the intelligent heart, without whose vitality we cannot fly.

Knowing this, I forgave all silently. I had learned lessons of silence from my native American Indian friends: Words carry their own weight and few know to use them wisely and sparingly. There is no more vital lesson than forgiveness–for me or any of my brothers and sisters on Earth. Removing the husk of pride, we remove karma's gravitational pull– the very dross that keeps us tethered to Earth when we could otherwise be raised to the heavens.

To graduate from the schoolroom of Earth, to receive the diploma signifying "Be with Us" in the higher octaves of life– is to receive the teachings, to wisely accept them and follow them. Now is the time for cosmic awareness, for increasing the sensitivity of the etheric body. For the mystics among us, Morya puts it thus:

The approaching time must put at the disposal of every sensitive spirit the tripod of Pythia.

Lest the reader think me coarse throughout this *Ode*– due in part to my vivid reenactments of earthly pleasure– it is time to explain: What I came to understand of the spirit's ecstasies, I learned first through my body, through the language of the heart. The chamber of the heart is the sacred place which houses the deepest sensations known to us on this Earth plane. Without allowing the full experience of the heart as it undergoes the earthly pleasures, one has little reference to the heaven world. As an initiate on the path so desirous of touching the Heaven world, I first had to touch the depths of my heart– to know the *feeling* coming from inside the sacred chamber. I found for myself two ways to *feel* and therefore to *know* the wisdom that waited for me inside that chamber: Kriya Yoga was one of them.

The second and most precious way to wisdom I found through the *Key of Green*, the nature kingdom, where my truest loving awaited its full blossoming. As a child I had meditated on flowers and trees; as an adult my heart was brimming full of that *Green Love*. In Kriya, I found myself in a graduated state of eternal *Green* ecstasy, quickly losing interest in sense activities which yielded less than the infinite ROI–the multidimensional bliss of the *Green mantissa*! With this kind of return, I could *feel* vestiges of the promised land brightening each day with thoughts more radiant than yesterday, adding interest to the future yield.

Radiant thoughts yield radiant vibrations in the body, harmonizing the electronic light making up our individual musical composition. Increasing in sensitivity to *all* strings of the great *Symphony of the One Life* unified by threads of the Antahkarana– I return to the keyboard where I began by practicing scales through the octaves of life.

Musing on my Father's song of life existential, I sing of that which I know will raise me to flight up the octaves. Together with nature I will sing my descant from inside nature's heart which is also mine. In *The Key of Green* I will sing: *I feel, therefore I AM*.

www.ingramcontent.com/pod-product-compliance
Lightning Source LLC
Chambersburg PA
CBHW031834090426
42741CB00005B/243